Focus on Life

Focus on Life

James P Taylor
BA   MEd

John Murray

Printed in Great Britain by Martins of Berwick

British Library Cataloguing in Publication Data

Taylor, James Peter
Focus on life.
1. Sociology – Addresses, essays, lectures
I. Title
300'.8   HM19

ISBN 0-7195-3800-9

Preface

Freedom is not merely the chance to do as one pleases; neither is it merely the opportunity to choose between set alternatives. Freedom is, first of all, the chance to formulate the available choices, to argue over them—and then, the opportunity to choose.

C. Wright Mills, *The Sociological Imagination*

It has been said that the secret of learning lies in the ability to pose the right sort of questions. There can be no doubt that, in relation to the art of living, the best sort of answers to those questions will be the ones we discover for ourselves.

This book, therefore, does not present any form of dogma. It is primarily a book of questions and statements of differing shades of opinion presented as a stimulus to discussion. It is designed for use in the upper forms of secondary schools and in further education, and may be used as a study in itself or to complement any syllabus of social, moral or religious education. The discussions should also prove particularly valuable for the new schemes of education in personal and social relationships which are now being developed in many colleges and schools.

Important aspects of life from birth onwards are introduced by means of extracts from works of biography, fiction, poetry and drama. The purpose of these extracts is threefold:

(a) to stimulate initial interest,
(b) to form a basis for each discussion,
(c) to illustrate the problems and concepts in terms of practical living.

Other questions and opinions may well occur within each discussion group. It is one of the aims of the book to stimulate them.

A detailed contents list is given so that material may be readily selected for any chosen topic. The social science concepts which are involved in the subject matter of each chapter also appear in the contents list. This will permit a choice of extracts which may serve to illustrate and make real the abstract theory which is a necessary part of social science examination courses.

J. P. T.

Contents

*Social Science concepts which are illustrated by the subject matter
of the chapter

1 Childhood

Socialisation   Significant others

Early influences

'Give me the child for the first five years and he is mine for life.'

The above quotation is well known. We are not sure who first said it. It is a claim, however, that we are made into the kind of people we are by the environment into which we are born. We are fashioned into shape, like vessels of clay, by those who look after us whilst we are still helpless babies. Some claim that this process begins before birth. They say we are being taught how to live even in our mother's womb. The impressions we gain in early childhood remain with us for the rest of our days.

Can this be true? How important is our childhood to us? Are we truly the products of our environment alone? Can our lives be 'set' in this way without our even being aware of it?

Security

Laurie Lee is an author who is able to recall many of the events of his very early years. In *Cider with Rosie* he describes the great sense of security he still remembers which arose from the loving relationship with his mother at the age of three.

I was still young enough then to be sleeping with my Mother, which to me seemed life's whole purpose. We slept together in the first-floor bedroom on a flock-filled mattress in a bed of brass rods and curtains. Alone, at that time, of all the family, I was her chosen dream companion, chosen from all for her extra love; my right, so it seemed to me.

1

So in the ample night and the thickness of her hair I consumed my fattened sleep, drowsed and nuzzling to her warmth of flesh, blessed by her bed and safety. From the width of the house and the separation of the day, we two then lay joined alone. That darkness to me was like the fruit of sloes, heavy and ripe to the touch. It was a darkness of bliss and simple languor, when all edges seemed rounded, apt and fitting; and the presence for whom one had moaned and hungered was found not to have fled after all.

My Mother, freed from her noisy day, would sleep like a happy child, humped in her nightdress, breathing innocently, and making soft drinking sounds in the pillow. In her flights of dream she held me close, like a parachute to her back; or rolled and enclosed me with her great tired body so that I was snug as a mouse in a hayrick.

They were deep and jealous, those wordless nights, as we curled and muttered together, like a secret I held through the waking day which set me above all others. It was for me alone that the night came down, for me the prince of her darkness, when only I would know the huge helplessness of her sleep, her dead face and her blind bare arms. At dawn, when she rose and stumbled back to the kitchen, even then I was not wholly deserted, but rolled into the valley her sleep had left, lay deep in its smell of lavender, deep on my face to sleep again in the nest she had made my own.

The sharing of her bed at that three-year-old time I expected to last for ever. I had never known, or could not recall, any night spent away from her. But I was growing fast; I was no longer the baby; brother Tony lay in wait in his cot. When I heard the first whispers of moving me to the boys' room, I simply couldn't believe it. Surely my Mother would never agree? How could she face night without me?

My sisters began by soothing and flattering; they said, 'You're a grown big man.' 'You'll be sleeping with Harold and Jack,' they said. 'Now what d'you think of that?' What was I supposed to think?—to me it seemed outrageous. I affected a brainstorm and won a few extra nights, my last nights in that downy bed. Then the girls changed their tune: 'It'll only be for a bit. You can come back to Mum later on.' I didn't quite believe them, but Mother was silent, so I gave up the struggle and went.

I was never recalled to my Mother's bed again. It was my

2

first betrayal, my first dose of ageing hardness, my first lesson in the gentle, merciless rejection of women. Nothing more was said, and I accepted it. I grew a little tougher, a little colder, and turned my attention more towards the outside world, which by now was emerging visibly through the mist.

From *Cider with Rosie* by Laurie Lee

1 What are the earliest memories you have of your own childhood? Which people do you remember best from those days?

2 Make a list of events or influences in early childhood which you think may cause a child to feel (a) secure or (b) insecure.

3 What sort of adult personality is likely to develop from (a) an insecure childhood or (b) an over-protected childhood?

4 Why do you think that the first five years of life are stressed as being so important? How far do you agree that a child's future is largely determined in those years?

5 In shaping our personalities, what influences do you think become important *after* the age of five?

Sadness or joy?

In the poem 'Prayer before Birth', from which the following lines are taken, the unborn child in the womb is pleading for mercy from the world it is about to enter. It sees itself as the helpless victim of a world which can be so good and yet so evil. It asks for the protection of those who will care for it.

I am not yet born; console me.
I fear that the human race may with tall walls wall me,
  with strong drugs dope me, with wise lies lure me,
    on black racks rack me, in blood-baths roll me.

I am not yet born; provide me
With water to dandle me, grass to grow for me, trees to talk
  to me, sky to sing to me, birds and a white light
    in the back of my mind to guide me.

I am not yet born; forgive me
For the sins that in me the world shall commit, my words
  when they speak me, my thoughts when they think me,
    my treason engendered by traitors beyond me,
      my life when they murder by means of my
        hands, my death when they live me.

I am not yet born; rehearse me
In the parts I must play and the cues I must take when
  old men lecture me, bureaucrats hector me, mountains
    frown at me, lovers laugh at me, the white
      waves call me to folly and the desert calls
        me to doom and the beggar refuses
          my gift and my children curse me.

I am not yet born; O hear me,
Let not the man who is beast or who thinks he is God
  come near me.

Louis MacNeice

6 Do you agree that a young baby is born as a helpless victim—a 'blank sheet' on which the world will write? Does the child bring nothing of its own into the world?

7 Another poet has written that the young child enters this world 'trailing clouds of glory'. Is a child born with a tendency to be good? Or with a tendency to be bad? If both, is one stronger than the other?

8 We often speak of the joys of parenthood. Do you enjoy 'baby-sitting'? What qualities do young children possess which can bring joy and happiness to those around them? What is it about babies that you find attractive or unattractive?

9 In what ways can a new baby make family life (a) happier or (b) more difficult?

10 Is everyone fitted for parenthood? Are there some people who are just not suitable? Or can anyone be a good and happy parent? Should any steps be taken to prevent some people from having children?

True or false?

These are statements to help you think about your own ideas and opinions. You will find similar groups of statements in other chapters. You may consider that some of them are not completely true or completely false. In some cases it may not be possible to give a definite answer without further information. If so, state what further information you would like to have.

11 Raising a family

(a) Raising a family is a natural instinct; only inadequate parents need to attend places like Child Welfare Clinics.

(b) All married couples should have children if they really want their marriage to be a happy one.

(c) The ideal family has two children, one boy and one girl.

(d) Family rows in front of young children help to prepare them for life.

(e) It is wrong for a mother to slap a child as a form of correction.

(f) The father is just as important as the mother in the care of young children.

(g) Children can be well taken care of by others while their mother goes out to work.

(h) If husbands and wives display their love and affection for each other it will make their children feel secure.

(i) Television can today take the place of story-telling and reading to young children.

(j) People should not have children unless they are sure they can afford them.

(k) A child should always feel that it can turn to one parent for support against the other.

(l) The joys of bringing up a family far outweigh the hard work and sacrifice involved.

Points of view

12 Parenthood and society

(a) Most people would accept that a child cannot be left to develop on its own from birth. It must be trained to conform to some acceptable standards of social behaviour. Such standards are included in the 'culture' of any particu-

5

lar society. If they were not passed on to the next generation, the society would break up and cease to exist.

Parents are in a special position in passing on this culture. No one else has such power and influence over their children. Parents cannot help imposing their own values and beliefs, either directly or indirectly. The way they live their day-to-day life is itself a statement of their values.

For many people, parenthood is, therefore, perhaps the most important task they will ever undertake. The future of the nation itself depends on the quality of its parents and the stability of family life. Every government should, therefore, give top priority to support for the family.

Do you agree? Or do we ask too much of parents? Are there better ways of bringing up children outside the family? Should other organisations—for example, the school—take over more of the responsibilities now held by parents?

(b) Here is a list of some of the means by which society seeks to help parents:

> Health Visitor Service
> Child Guidance and Welfare Clinics
> Welfare Baby Foods
> Marriage Guidance Councils
> Family Planning Clinics
> Home Help Service
> Meals and Milk in School
> Courses in 'Parentcraft'
> School Medical and Dental Services
> Nursery Schools
> Day Nurseries for working mothers
> Financial help:
>> Family Allowance
>> Maternity Allowance and Grant
>> Supplementary Benefits (Free prescriptions,
>> Family Income Supplement, etc.)

Do all the above services operate well in your neighbourhood? You could make it a group project to find out. Which of them, in your opinion, give the help which is most needed? Do you think any of them are unnecessary? Can you suggest any improvements which could be made?

2 Family

Nuclear family Social role and status
Social change

A family quarrel

Spring and Port Wine is a play by Bill Naughton about the stresses which occur in a modern working-class home when Rafe Crompton, the old-fashioned father of the family, insists on sticking rigidly to his traditional values. The action centres on what happens when Hilda, his nineteen-year-old daughter, does not wish to eat a herring for her tea.

Daisy is Rafe's wife. Harold, a weaver, and Florence, a teacher, are the eldest son and daughter of the family. Wilfred, a mechanic, is eighteen and the youngest member.

It is Friday evening. The week's work is done and the family is sitting round the tea-table.

Hilda. I say, Mum, I really don't fancy my herring—if you don't mind.

Daisy. No, of course not, love! What would you like instead? I've got some nice fresh eggs.

Harold. Aye, with some streaky rashers.

Hilda. No, just an egg.

Harold. Sunny side up?

Hilda. Done on both sides. But wait till you're finished, Mum.

Daisy. It's all right, love—won't take me a minute. (*Rising.*) You must be ready for it after a day's work. . .

(*They think they have got away with it, but Rafe quietly beckons Daisy to sit.*)

Rafe. Hold on a minute, Mother. (*To Hilda.*) Is there something wrong with your herring?

Hilda. No, nothing wrong with it—only I don't feel like it.

Rafe. That's a lovely fresh herring, it's been done in best butter, and yet you have the nerve to sit there and say you don't feel like it.

Hilda. What else can I say if I don't?

Rafe. You can eat it and say nothing.

Harold. Well, that's asking a bit much, Dad!

Hilda. I'll just go and fry myself an egg, Mum!

Rafe. No, you won't.

Hilda. Why not?

Rafe. Because this is a home, not a cafeteria.

Hilda. I'm entitled to some choice over what I have for my tea—I'm bringing my share of money into the home.

Rafe. You don't think I thought less of you over all the years you never brought in a ha'penny? I'd as soon see the smiling face you had in them days than you were bringing twenty pounds a week home today.

Wilfred. Here, Dad, to save any bother, I'll eat our Hilda's herring.

Rafe. You'll do nothing of the sort. You get on with your own tea.

Daisy (not put out). Dad—it wouldn't take a second to fry an egg.

Rafe. There's no fried eggs coming on the scene.

Hilda. Then there's no point in my waiting here. (*Rising.*) Excuse me, everbody—I'll just go upstairs . . .

Rafe (quietly). No you won't. Sit down.

Hilda. What?

Rafe. I said sit down.

(*Hilda is undecided. Daisy gives her a pleading look.*)

Pigs leave their troughs when it suits—but not civilised human beings.

(*Wilfred gives Hilda a look of sympathetic support, Florence gives her a reproving glance. Harold continues to eat with an air of detached interest about the outcome. Daisy does not want trouble, but gives Hilda a comforting, motherly look.*)

Daisy. Dad—I'll just . . .

(*Rafe remains oddly above it all, continuing to eat naturally as he talks. Hilda catches Daisy's look and sits down, but away from the table.*)

Rafe. No, you won't, Mother. They were never spoilt when young—it 'ud be a pity to start now. One day, young woman, you may realise what words like home and family mean. A

8

man and woman marry, they have children, feed and tend 'em, work for 'em, guide, aye, and love 'em.

Hilda. Just as they ought.

Rafe. Aye, I agree—as they ought. Over the years they try to make a home for those children, not just a furnished place to live in, but a home, mark you, with some culture. But do those children thank you? Well, perhaps some do—mostly they don't. They take you an' your home for granted. Well, there's nobody taking me for granted.

Hilda. I don't see why I should eat that herring if I don't want it . . .

Rafe (detached). Then I'll tell you one reason why—as comes to mind at the moment. Pass me the bread, Florence, please. Have you ever heard of the Hunger Marchers?

(Florence passes the bread. Rafe takes a piece.)

Hilda. Yes, folk out in foreign countries.

Rafe. I mean folk in this country. Thank you, Florence. *(Eating as he talks.)* Something you never realised.

Wilfred. Must have been in the old days, Dad.

Rafe. It was when your brother Harold here was a babe in arms and your mother was six months carrying our Florence. That's when it was. I was out of work at the time. One day we set off to Queen's Park to have a picnic. We'd some flour cakes and a bottle of cold tea. On Chorley Old Road we suddenly came on the Hunger Marchers marching along.

Wilfred. Who were they, Dad, and where were they off to?

Rafe. They were men down from the Clydeside. Men who'd been out of work for years, and had seen their wives and families go hungry. A band of them got together to walk the four hundred miles' stretch to the Houses of Parliament. Mother, do you remember their feet, all sore and bandaged up?

Daisy. Yes—and I remember their faces. They were singing, weren't they?

Rafe. Nay, not singing, Mother, whistling. I don't think they had the strength to sing, but by heck they could whistle.

Daisy. Yes, they were whistling Loch Lomond.

Rafe (to Hilda). We were standing there as they went by. I can hear 'em this minute. Your mother nudged me as one weary-looking chap came up. The next thing she'd taken the flour cakes from under my arm and handed them to him. And on they went. That didn't happen in foreign countries; it happened here. And once you've lived through it you don't forget it.

Hilda. But it can't happen these days.

Harold. Them times are gone for ever.

Rafe. That's what I thought before it happened to me.

Harold. You can't have another depression—they've got economic planning that makes it impossible.

Rafe. If the Government suddenly decided there were too many cars on the road—and put a curb on production—there could be thousands out of work next month.

Florence. What happened to you, Dad?

Rafe (eating as he talks). At the mill where I'd worked from a boy they'd made me engine tenter over Nellie, as we called her. I thought I'd a job for life, looking after the engine. Till one clever official up in London decided it would pay them to close down a few hundred mills and have the machinery broken up. Economic Planning, see.

Wilfred. Why, Dad?

Rafe. Hitler were paying a big price for scrap iron, needed all he could get. It was a chance not to be missed. So they gave us all a week's notice, shut the mill down one Friday, and on the Monday after they had scrap men in, smashing the machinery up.

Florence. Was it hard to get work in those times?

Rafe. It wasn't all that easy—with well over half the country out of work, searching for jobs. It took me eighteen months. Hardly a week went by but they'll pull some poor chap out of yon canal down the road. *(He thumbs over his shoulder.)*

Daisy. Aye, and many a poor woman too.

Wilfred. And did they smash her up—your engine, Nellie?

Rafe. What else? I told you Hitler urgently needed all the scrap-iron he could lay hands on for making guns and shells and bombs. Mind you, we got most of it back around nineteen-forty.

Hilda. Hitler! Why bring him up? That's all a thing of the past—it's another world.

Rafe. It might be to you—but it's not to me.

Hilda. Well, I still don't see what all this has got to do with a herring.

(Wilfred nods in agreement. Rafe silences him with a look.)

10

Rafe. Look at your mother—in those days she was a young woman, and a bonny woman, not much older than you are now—and she hadn't had a decent meal in months. She would have given thanks to God for that good wholesome food on your plate. But she was lucky to get a bit of bread and dripping, or the odd slice of potted meat. (*With a rising outburst.*) So I won't have you sit there in front of me and see you make little of good food! Because you're making little of the life we've had to live! And millions like us.

Daisy. Dad—calm yourself.

Rafe. I can't stand the way young people are today—all for themselves, and all for the present, as though the past didn't exist.

Daisy (*always achieving a balance of sympathy*). More tea, Dad?

Rafe. No, thank you, Mother—not just now. (*Rising*) But there is one thing you can do for me—have that herring of our Hilda's safely put on one side—and you serve it to her, and nothing else, at every meal—until she eats it! I'm having no more sloppy living under my roof. (*He picks up his jacket.*)

Hilda. I won't eat it . . .

Rafe. We'll see—because you'll eat nothing at my table until you have. (*He picks up his collar and tie.*)

Hilda. I won't touch it! Not if it's there till Kingdom come!

Rafe. Right, we'll see the outcome. I'll go and get ready for my union meeting. If you get the better of me you'll be the first in this house who has. Mother, I'm relying on you over that herring.

Daisy. I'll get it out of the way at once, Dad.

(*Rafe exits up centre. Daisy has seen quarrels come and go and doesn't take them too seriously. She gives Hilda a pat, then exits to the kitchen with the herring.*)

Harold (*to Hilda*). Don't worry—they'll be comin' to take him away in the yellow cab very soon, the way he's going on. He's obsessed.

Florence (*angrily*). Don't you be so stupid!

Harold. What—a scene like that all over a herring? He must be mad.

Florence. It's not over a herring—it's over a principle. You've got to have some order in a home.

Hilda. Oh, shut up, our Florence! You're as bad as him.

Wilfred. Now then, now then, let's not row . . .

Florence. If she had eaten her tea there'd have been no row. She's full of likes and dislikes lately.

Harold. She's been on the port wine, hasn't she!

(*There is a knock on the front door.*)

Sumdy at door, Wilf!

Florence (*rising*). It's all right—I'll go. You know Dad detests anybody fussing over their food—not eating what's put in front of them. With half the world starving.

(*Florence exits up centre to the front door.*)

Hilda. Dad—Dad—Dad—you'd think he was the only one in the house!

Wilfred (*going to Hilda and putting his arm round her*). Take no notice, love.

Harold. I'll lay you two-to-one you'll eat that herring.

Hilda. I will hell as like!

Harold. I bet you.

Hilda. You're on.

From *Spring and Port Wine* by Bill Naughton

1 Who was to blame for this family conflict? Rafe or Hilda?

(a) Rafe was to blame. By insisting that Hilda should eat the herring he was making a most unreasonable demand. The matter was a trivial one and there was no compelling reason why Hilda should have forced herself to eat something she disliked. If Rafe had really loved his daughter he could not have subjected her to such humiliation. Moreover, Hilda was nineteen and entitled to the dignity and freedom of an independent adult. Rafe would never have treated an adult guest in such a way.

(b) Hilda was to blame. She should have realised that her father was a product of his generation who, because of past experiences, found it impossible to tolerate the waste of food. If she had really loved her father she would have made some effort to eat the herring in order to keep the peace. The standards and values of the parents must be respected in their own home, and children, even when adult, should conform to them as long as they live there.

What do you think?

Family roles

2 Do you agree that there are definite roles to be filled by parents and children in family life? Are there some roles for which one partner in a marriage is more fitted by nature than the other?

Details are given below of the traditional roles which have been followed for many years in homes like that of Rafe and Daisy. What changes (if any) would you make in the light of your experience of modern living?

Mother: shopping
preparation of meals
housework
general care of children—health, cleanliness, etc.
sewing and mending
allocation of housekeeping money
arranging family entertainment, outings, children's
parties

Father: outside employment to earn money
supervision of family budget
payment of all expenses apart from housekeeping
repair and decoration of house
repair and maintenance of car
discipline of children

Children: obedience to parents
household duties as allocated

3 How much assistance in the home should older children be called upon to give (a) while still at school and (b) when out at work?

4 Should children who are earning an adult wage and living at home pay the same rent they would have to pay if living in lodgings?

Modern youth

5 In *Spring and Port Wine,* Rafe gives his opinion that the young people of today are selfish and think only of themselves. Statements like that have always been made by someone about every new generation. We often hear older people claim that, in their

young days, they were much better than today's youth. The Greek teacher, Plato, said that the young of Athens in his day lived a life of ease. They had bad manners, they gobbled their food, and they showed no respect to their parents. That was about 2,400 years ago!

(a) Is it possible to compare one generation with a previous one?
(b) Have we the necessary information to make valid judgements about which one was better?
(c) Can we tell how previous generations would have acted in the very different social conditions of a new age?
(d) What are the strengths of young people today compared with the past? For example, are they more honest and open-minded, less afraid to say what they really think?

What are their weaknesses? It is said that they are too concerned with money and material things such as clothes, record-players, motor-bikes, etc. Do you agree?

6 In what ways would you say that our society today is more just and caring than it ever used to be—for example, in the care of the sick, the handicapped and the aged?

Do young people play any part in helping to keep it so?

7 Rafe also speaks of the hunger marches of the 1930s and the great courage and spirit shown by the men taking part. The standard and quality of our lives have much improved since those days. But has that meant that we are now less strong in character?

Does the present generation show the same courage and spirit today but in different ways?

Or have higher living standards made us 'soft' and less willing to make sacrifices when they become necessary?

Does the human spirit *need* to face hardship, or even disaster, before it can grow strong?

Points of view

8 *The generation gap*

(a) *The children*

Our way of life is constantly and rapidly changing with modern technology. The world of today's youth is very different from the one our parents knew when they were

A new way of life? Or just part of growing up?

young. This is something no one can alter. It can never again be 'like it was in the old days'. The tastes and values of the two generations are bound to clash. What we need is more tolerance.

Today, we can earn much more money much earlier than our parents could. This makes us more independent. We can 'do our own thing'. But far too much fuss is made about trivial things like our forms of entertainment and our clothes. Fashions have always changed in such things and they always will. You will always get a few people who go to extremes. The majority of young people act quite sensibly.

In the things that really matter we are better informed, through television and the other media, than any previous generation has been. This makes us question those who hold power, and that includes parents. We want to know why. It is not enough to expect us to obey given rules. We must be given explanations and be convinced that what is being asked of us is reasonable. That is how real progress can be made in social life, and that is what freedom is all about.

15

(b) *The parents*

We agree that society is changing rapidly, but that means that we need even more knowledge and experience of life in order to make choices which will be mature and sound. There are some values which do not change. Lessons which have been learnt in the hard school of life need to be passed on to future generations.

It is important to give explanations, and there should always be frank discussions in the family. But young people cannot be expected to see the force of every argument and, in the end, they must trust their parents to act in everyone's best interests. Those parents will often be trying to protect them from dangers of which they are not yet fully aware, but which could cause them great misery in later life.

Freedom is what we all want, but it carries with it obligations. Freedom does not mean licence to do as we please. It must always make allowance for the rights of others. Could it be said that the young people of today are asking for too much freedom too soon?

What do you think?

3 Education

A good school?

Afternoon quiet. Darkening sky. Cloud skittering low in thickening hues.

The rooms along the front of the school were lighted: rooms 1 to 6, two bright blocks divided by foyer and offices. From the road, looking through the railings across the grass, silent pictures from room to room; same story, different players; the teacher at the front, the profiles of the window row. Rooms 6 and 5, teachers seated. 4, standing at the board. The Deputy's office, the Deputy at his desk. Foyer dim, deserted, like the Headmaster's room next to it. The secretary in her office, straight-backed, fingers dancing on the keys. Room 3, empty, lights left on. Room 2, Billy half-way down the row. Windows closed, top panes misting over.

The class was quiet, working; the teacher reading, looking up each time he turned a page. The atmosphere was heavy. The air stunk of sour milk and sweat. Billy eased himself down in his chair and stretched his legs under the desk. He lay his left arm along the radiator and closed his eyes.

The scuffle of a turning page. A shifting chair. A whisper. A giggle. And a cough. All isolated, exaggerated sounds.

'Casper.'

A voice from the gods.

'Casper!'

Billy sat up white-faced, staring like somebody laid too long. He stretched, fingers linked, joints going off like jumping crackers.

'Get on with your work lad.' Then back to his book.

Billy dipped his pen and leaned over his book, shading his eyes with his left hand.

17

Divide 42174 by 781.

Pen poised, nib pointing at the page. The ink skin in the nib-hole burst, scattered spots between the turquoise lines. Billy's eyelids began to droop. His elbow began to slide along the desk, his body after it, until the lip of the desk lid stopped his chest and made him open his eyes. He changed elbows, snuggled his shins up to the radiator and settled again, his glazed eyes fixed on the window. Clouding window. He raised his hand and drew his nib down through the cloud, scratching a course as clear as water. His hand stayed limp on the sill. The nib rusted, and the inkspots on his exercise book dried. . .

Billy opened his eyes and stared at the window as though listening to it. The whole pane was obscure. He wiped a hole in the mist and peered through it. Nobody there. Just a passing car, the smudged glass blurring its outline and spangling its lamps like tears.

'Anything to report, Casper?'

Billy turned to the front.

'Never mind what's going off out there, get on with your work, lad.'

Divide 42174 by 781.

From *A Kestrel for a Knave* by Barry Hines

1 What makes a good school? Put the following points into your order of importance and compare the opinions of your group.

(a) social activities—discoes, camps, holidays
(b) sporting competitions—football, netball, hockey, athletics
(c) school societies and clubs—music, drama, debate, chess
(d) strict enforcement of rules for good behaviour in and out of of the classroom
(e) friendships with other pupils
(f) team spirit—the feeling of belonging to a community with a common purpose
(g) good personal relationships between pupils and teachers
(h) teachers who can make their lessons interesting
(i) good personal relationships between parents and teachers
(j) good examination results and job qualifications
(k) involvement in the surrounding community—neighbourhood visits, care of old people
(l) an effective say in all school affairs by the pupils

How important are examination results to a good school?

Rules and punishment

2 In your present school which school rules do you consider to be
(a) necessary and (b) unnecessary?

3 Why do you think most school rules are obeyed by pupils?

(a) They are afraid of being found out and punished if they
disobey
(b) They are convinced of their necessity
(c) They believe school authorities should be obeyed at all
times
(d) They don't think much about it; it just causes less fuss to
obey

4 Is punishment necessary in schools? If so, what form should it
take and for what offences should it be given? Why was corporal
punishment so prevalent in the past?

5 What is the greatest benefit you think you have obtained from
your school life?

Disadvantage

Barry Hines's book *A Kestrel for a Knave*, from which the above extract is taken, and the film *Kes*, which was based on the book, seek to show that the type of education given by our schools is quite inappropriate to the lives of some of their pupils. These are the children who come from 'disadvantaged' homes—children like Timothy Winters.

Timothy Winters comes to school
With eyes as wide as a football-pool,
Ears like bombs and teeth like splinters:
A blitz of a boy is Timothy Winters.

His belly is white, his neck is dark,
And his hair is an exclamation-mark.
His clothes are enough to scare a crow
And through his britches the blue winds blow.

When teacher talks he won't hear a word
And he shoots down dead the arithmetic-bird,
He licks the patterns off his plate
And he's not even heard of the Welfare State.

Timothy Winters has bloody feet
And he lives in a house on Suez Street,
He sleeps in a sack on the kitchen floor
And they say there aren't boys like him any more.

Old Man Winters likes his beer
And his missus ran off with a bombardier,
Grandma sits in the grate with a gin
And Timothy's dosed with an aspirin.

The Welfare Worker lies awake
But the law's as tricky as a ten-foot snake,
So Timothy Winters drinks his cup
And slowly goes on growing up.

At Morning Prayers the Master helves
For children less fortunate than ourselves,
And the loudest response in the room is when
Timothy Winters roars 'Amen!'

So come one angel, come on ten:
Timothy Winters says 'Amen
Amen amen amen amen.'
Timothy Winters, Lord.

Amen.

Charles Causley

helves: appeals to God

6 Read again the poem 'Prayer before Birth' on page 3. Does it express the same ideas as the poem about Timothy Winters? Is Timothy Winters the sort of child Louis MacNeice had in mind when he wrote 'Prayer before Birth'? What reasons can be given to explain why some parents show such little love for their own children?

7 What sort of help can a school give to 'disadvantaged' children? What do such children really need from a school? Should they be treated just the same as anyone else? Or is it better if they are taught in special classes?

8 Which is the better form of organisation in any school— streaming or mixed ability classes?

9 Is it possible for a good school to make up for a bad home?

10 What sort of things have parents to do if their children are to succeed and be happy at school? How necessary are the following in this respect?

(a) membership of Parent/Teacher Associations and atten-
    dance at the meetings
(b) attendance at school social functions, open days, sports
    days etc.
(c) meetings with individual teachers to discuss progress
(d) public meetings in school to discuss the syllabus and
    methods of teaching
(e) automatic support of their children in any grievance
    against the school
(f) willingness to help children with homework
(g) giving of money for school funds, extra books, etc.

21

Boarding-school or home life? Senior pupils at a British public school relax in their own bar.

11 What are the advantages and disadvantages of a boarding-school education? Which of the following reflects your view of it?

(a) never a good thing and cannot be a substitute for any kind of home life
(b) better than having to live with relatives or in a children's home
(c) provides an educational experience from which all children could derive benefit at some period in their school lives

12 Has a government any right to make a period at boarding-school a compulsory element in state education?

Points of view

13 *The teacher*

In the passage given below, a writer describes his favourite teacher. The writer is very practical. He sees the competent teacher as being good at passing on knowledge and skill to the pupils. He does not want teachers who make a big display of being reasonable ('sanctimonious') or even friendly ('camaraderie'). He does not care what sort of persons they are so long as they can teach. This is what brings 'gratification' to the pupils, a sense of having achieved something, even if it is only in the effort they have made. He points out that foolish 'evangelists of education', those who talk a lot about it and claim to have the answers, have not yet realised this.

What do you think?

Miss O'Neill did not try to please us. She did not try to like us. She certainly made no effort to make us like her. She valued results more than affection, and, I suspect, respect more than popularity. She was not endowed with either loving or lovable attributes, and she did not bother regretting it or denying it or trying to compensate for it. She went about her task with a forthright 'I want' or 'You go' instead of the sanctimonious 'Shall we?' She concentrated solely on the transmission of her knowledge and the transferring of her skill.

I think Miss O'Neill understood what foolish evangelists of education are bound to rediscover: that drill and discipline are not detestable; that whether they know it or not, children prefer competence to 'personality' in a teacher; that communication is more significant than camaraderie; that what is hard to master gives students special rewards (pride, self-respect, the unique gratification of having succeeded) precisely because difficulties have been conquered, ramparts scaled, battles won; that there may be no easy road at all to learning some things, and no 'fascinating' or 'fun' way of learning some things really well.

From *People I Have Loved, Known or Admired* by Leo Rosten

What do you look for in a 'good' teacher?
Can you describe one you have known?
If not, can you describe one you would like to have known?

4 Work

Culture   Alienation   Social control

Toil and drudgery

The tiny island of Tristan da Cunha is no more than a sleeping volcano rising from the ocean bed far out in the South Atlantic. In the year 1961 it represented the whole world to its 270 inhabitants. There they lived their primitive lives in almost complete isolation. Then, in October of that year, the volcano suddenly erupted into life.

For three days and nights the Tristanites struggled for survival as their island was destroyed by the force of a series of shattering explosions. The devastation became too much and they had at last to abandon their homes and allow themselves to be evacuated. Eventually the displaced people were brought to England and assisted in the attempt to settle in a new land.

In spite of the fact that many of the islanders found work here, they were making desperate efforts to go back to Tristan within one year of their arrival. Great dangers still existed on the island but, with only one or two exceptions, the settlers voted to return to their volcano as soon as they possibly could.

Here are some of the comments which they made before they left England:

'Don't think that we're not grateful for what you have done for us. It's just that we can't breathe freely. In England people seem nervous from the moment they are born till the moment they die, and this nervousness, this continued striving, seems meaningless to us Tristanites. People don't get time to dream, to think, to enjoy peace and quiet and the wonders of life—the sea, the mountains, the fresh air. You have only one god, and that god's name is money. You try to get exactly the same as your neighbour—and a bit more—and if you can't live up to his standard you think you ought to feel unhappy.'

24

'Englishmen only work to make money. They are slaves for eight hours a day so that they can behave like fools for the rest of the twenty-four hours. We enjoy work for work's sake. We look forward to planting potatoes, to fencing the fields and to getting the cattle under control. Every time we are out fishing at sea we feel a thrill. But there's not much of a thrill in passing bricks up to a man standing above you on a ladder.'

from *Back to Tristan* by Arne Falk-Rønne

1 Do you agree with the Tristanites?

(a) Most of our work is monotonous drudgery from which we get no joy
(b) We become unhappy if we think our standard of living is below that of our neighbour
(c) We work only for money which is the centre of our lives

Are these comments on life in England fair?

2 The poet D. H. Lawrence had this to say about 'wage-slaves':

All That We Have Is Life

All that we have, while we live, is life;
and if you don't live during your life, you are a piece of
    dung.
And work is life, and life is lived in work
unless you're a wage slave.
While a wage slave works, he leaves life aside
and stands there a piece of dung.
Men should refuse to be lifelessly at work.
Men should refuse to be heaps of wage-earning dung.
Men should refuse to work at all, as wage-slaves.
Men should demand to work for themselves, of themselves,
    and put their life in it.
For if a man has no life in his work, he is mostly a heap
    of dung.

Work may be a self-fulfilling activity for some, but is this possible for everyone? Can you think of work which is essential but also dull, routine or dirty? How can a man put his life into such work?

25

3 What chance do you think you have of finding a job which will be varied and interesting?

A just wage

4 Is it unjust that an entertainer, for example, can command a fee for one hour's performance which is several times greater than a nurse's salary for a whole year? Is it possible to ensure that we all earn exactly what we are worth?

5 Which of the following should carry most weight in calculating earnings?

> value to the community
> amount of study needed to qualify
> conditions of work—hours, difficulty, fatigue, etc.
> amount of responsibility
> financial profit

Job satisfaction

6 The following factors are likely to affect the degree of satisfaction you feel with your job. Select those factors which would be most important to you in this respect and put them in order of priority:

(a) Achievement—the sense of achievement you obtain from work that fulfils you and is socially useful.
(b) Recognition—others recognise and acknowledge the value and importance of your performance.
(c) Responsibility—the extent to which you can act on your own initiative as opposed to being under constant supervision.
(d) Advancement—the degree of promotion possible.
(e) Relationships—(i) the attitude and friendliness of those you work with.
(f) Relationships—(ii) the attitude and friendliness of those in authority.
(g) Conditions—the physical conditions under which you work.
(h) Duration—the hours of work and amount of holiday.
(i) Salary.

Factory workers hurry home. What does job satisfaction really mean?

True or false?

7 The new age of employment

(a) Eventually we will enter a new age of leisure when computers and other machines will have removed all toil from our lives.

(b) Toil and effort in work can have a very beneficial effect upon us.

(c) Some people actually prefer simple and monotonous work and are only too glad to choose it.

(d) It is a fact of life that no one has a job which is free from all drudgery.

(e) It's my money. If I've earned it I'm entitled to spend it as I wish.

(f) There should be an upper and a lower limit to all earnings.

(g) A business should share its profits with the workers who have helped to make them.

(h) There is nothing wrong in 'going slow' in order to prevent redundancies and unemployment.

(i) It is the government's responsibility to make sure that there is employment for everybody.

Points of view

8 Trade unions

(a) Under modern conditions every working man or woman has a duty to belong to a trade union and take an active interest in its affairs. It is wrong for workers to enjoy the benefits obtained for them by the union and yet opt out of their responsibility to give it support. Those who are not interested enough in their own future to attend meetings should abide by the decisions of those who are. Unity in the fight for justice is so important that if any workers refuse to join, then the union should prevent them from working in that trade.

Nobody can take away the right of workers to withdraw their labour. The ultimate weapon of strike action is the only form of power trade unions have which can counter the power of the employers. On the whole they have always used it in a responsible manner.

(b) Today, the unions are not fighting for existence as they were in their early days. They have now gained great power, and it must be used with proper consideration for the rights of others. The individual must remain free to follow his conscience and opt in or out of a trade union as he wishes. It may be a good thing for all workers to be in unions, but it is against basic freedom to force them to join by threatening that they will otherwise lose their right to work—the 'closed shop'.

Most workers now earn enough to pay for the essentials of life. They are right to seek an even higher standard of living. But this does not justify strikes, which can and do bring hardship and suffering to other members of the community, particularly the old and the sick. That is not responsible action. The end must justify the means. The benefits unions seek through strike action today are often out of all proportion to the suffering they cause to others.

What do you think?

5 Law

The need for law

King Henry VIII of England is well known for the fact that he had
six wives. Most people also know that his attempts to rid himself
of the first one were opposed by the Pope in Rome. At this time,
Henry's chief minister was a famous lawyer, Sir Thomas More.
More felt that he must support the Pope, and this brought him
into conflict with the King. The story of that conflict is told in the
play *A Man for all Seasons* by Robert Bolt.

As More fell from the King's favour, his life was in danger. The
King wanted his consent or his execution. More saw the 'law of
the land' as his great protection. He believed that if he could claim
that he had broken no law he would be safe. To More the written
law of England was sacred. He would not even use his power as a
minister to remove his own enemies, so long as they had not
broken any law.

In this scene from Bolt's play, More has just been visited in his
home by Rich, a man who could cause him great harm. As Rich
leaves, Alice (More's wife), Roper (his son-in-law) and Margaret
(his daughter) urge More to get rid of him.

(*Exit Rich. All watch him; the others turn to More, their faces alert.*)

Roper. Arrest him.
Alice. Yes!
More. For what?
Alice. He's dangerous!
Roper. For libel; he's a spy.
Alice. He is! Arrest him!
Margaret. Father, that man's bad.
More. There is no law against that.

29

Sir Thomas More, Chancellor of England. Pope or King? A case of conscience.

Roper. There is! God's law!

More. Then God can arrest him. . . .

Alice (exasperated, pointing after Rich). While you talk, he's gone!

More. And go he should if he was the Devil himself until he broke the law!

Roper. So now you'd give the Devil benefit of law!

More. Yes. What would you do? Cut a great road through the law to get after the Devil?

Roper. I'd cut down every law in England to do that!

More (roused and excited). Oh? (*Advances on Roper.*) And when the last law was down, and the Devil turned round on you—where would you hide, Roper, the laws all being flat. (*Leaves him.*) This country's planted thick with laws from coast to coast—Man's laws, not God's—and if you cut them down—and you're just the man to do it—d'you really think you could stand upright in the winds that would blow then? (*Quietly*) Yes, I'd give the Devil benefit of law, for my own safety's sake.

Roper. I have long suspected this; this is the golden calf; the law's your God.

More (wearily). Oh, Roper you're a fool, God's my god . . . (*Rather bitter*) But I find him rather too (*very bitter*) subtle . . . I don't know where he is nor what he wants.

Roper. My god wants service, to the end and unremitting; nothing else!

More (dry). Are you sure that's God?—He sounds like Moloch. But indeed it may be God—And whoever hunts for me, Roper, God or Devil, will find me hiding in the thickets of the law!

From *A Man for all Seasons* by Robert Bolt

1 Who makes the laws of England? Why have they the right to make them and to demand, under threat of punishment, that all citizens obey them?

2 Do you agree that the 'law of the land' is the most important means of protecting the rights and freedom of its citizens? Could any society exist without some form of law?

3 Do laws express the values which are held by a society? Must there always be a set of values which are agreed and acted upon by the majority of its members?

4 How do the laws of God differ from the laws of man? Study the Ten Commandments. If you disobey them in how many cases would you also be disobeying the law of the land?

Authority

5 Many people hold some form of authority, that is, they have a right to make rules or laws and to ask others to obey them. How many people, or groups of people, do you know who hold authority of some kind?

6 There are many questions which arise:

(a) Where does the right to hold authority come from?
(b) How do we decide whether someone's authority is lawful or unlawful?
(c) Have we a duty to obey all lawful authority?
(d) Are there limits to authority? Are there some things we cannot be asked to do?
(e) Are all lawful authorities equal? Or can one overrule another?

Consider each of the above questions in relation to the powers held by (i) parents, (ii) teachers, (iii) policemen, (iv) employers.

7 Are you ever placed in a position of authority?

The inhumanity of law

Laws cannot be written to cover every possible case which might arise. They can be applied in such a way that a particular individual suffers hardship and injustice. Laws can sometimes be inhuman. In the following passage from his famous novel *Tess of the D'Urbervilles*, Thomas Hardy gives us a good example.

There are Church laws about the conditions which are necessary before a minister may conduct a Christian burial. In the past they were often applied very rigidly. Even tiny infants who had died without being baptised could be refused a Christian burial. Many people believed that there would be no place in heaven for them.

Tess had given birth to an illegitimate child. Through a misunderstanding, for which she was not to blame, the baby died before it could be baptised by the vicar. Full of fear, Tess herself had performed a baptism on the child, as best she could, just before it died. Then, frantic with worry, she wanted to make certain that her baptism would be lawful and that her child could have a Christian burial as a citizen of heaven.

Tess, who mused on the christening a great deal wondered if it were doctrinally sufficient to secure a Christian burial for the child. Nobody could tell this but the parson of the parish, and he was a newcomer, and did not know her. She went to his house after dusk, and stood by the gate, but could not summon courage to go in. The enterprise would have been abandoned if she had not by accident met him coming homeward as she turned away. In the gloom she did not mind speaking freely.

'I should like to ask you something, sir.'

He expressed his willingness to listen, and she told the story of the baby's illness and the extemporised ordinance.[1]

'And now, sir,' she added earnestly, 'can you tell me this—will it be just the same for him as if you had baptised him?' . . .

The man and the ecclesiastic[2] fought within him, and the victory fell to the man.

'My dear girl,' he said, 'it will be just the same.'

'Then will you give him a Christian burial?' she asked quickly.

The Vicar felt himself cornered. Hearing of the baby's illness, he had conscientiously gone to the house after nightfall to perform the rite, and, unaware that the refusal to admit him had come from Tess's father and not from Tess, he could not allow the plea of necessity for its irregular administration.

'Ah—that's another matter,' he said.

'Another matter—why?' asked Tess, rather warmly.

'Well—I would willingly do so if only we two were concerned. But I must not—for certain reasons.'

'Just for once, sir!'

'Really I must not.'

'O sir!' She seized his hand as she spoke.

He withdrew it, shaking his head.

'Then I don't like you!' she burst out, 'and I'll never come to your church no more!'

'Don't talk so rashly.'

'Perhaps it will be just the same to him if you don't? . . . Will it be just the same? Don't for God's sake speak as saint to sinner, but as you yourself to me myself—poor me!'

How the Vicar reconciled his answer with the strict notions he supposed himself to hold on these subjects it is beyond a layman's power to tell, though not to excuse. Somewhat moved, he said in this case also:

'It will be just the same.'

So the baby was carried in a small deal box, under an ancient woman's shawl, to the churchyard that night, and buried by lantern-light, at the cost of a shilling and a pint of beer to the sexton, in that shabby corner of God's allotment where He lets the nettles grow, and where all unbaptised infants, notorious drunkards, suicides, and others of the conjecturally damned[3] are laid. In spite of the untoward surroundings, however, Tess bravely made a little cross of two laths and a piece of string, and having bound it with flowers, she stuck it up at the head of the grave one evening when she could enter the churchyard without being seen, putting at the foot also a bunch of the same flowers in a little jar of water to keep them alive. What matter was it that on the outside of the jar the eye of mere observation noted the words 'Keelwell's Marmalade'? The eye of maternal affection did not see them in its vision of higher things.

From *Tess of the D'Urbervilles* by Thomas Hardy

---

[1] 'the extemporised ordinance'—the attempt which Tess herself had made to baptise her baby.

[2] 'the man and the ecclesiastic'—as if he were two different persons: a human being with pity for Tess, and a churchman who must obey the laws of his church.

[3] 'the conjecturally damned'—those whom the Church seems to have written off as having no chance of heaven. Hardy uses this expression to show his own dismay at this inhuman application of law.

8 What do we mean by justice? Is it solely a matter of applying rules or laws? What do we mean when we say that something is legally right but morally wrong? How do we decide what is morally wrong?

9 Laws cannot be written to cover every case which can arise. Does this mean that some people will always have to suffer injustice? Which is more important: to make sure that laws and rules are obeyed; or to make sure that mercy and kindness are shown to the individual?

10 What are the dangers if we do not keep to the letter of the law? Who is entitled to say that a law or rule need not apply in a particular case?
Is a law weakened if exceptions are made to it?

11 Consider the following case:

> A pupil has been caught stealing money from other members of his class. The Headteacher lets him off with a warning. The rest of the class do not think this is punishment enough. They decide that no member of the class will speak to the guilty one. They will 'send him to Coventry' until he pays back all the stolen money.

Do you think the pupils have the right to take such action? What are the dangers of taking the law into your own hands?

Points of view

12 *Conscience*

In the end, Sir Thomas More was executed because his conscience would not allow him to accept the law that made King Henry the Head of the Church. Today, a sincere pacifist will go to prison rather than perform military service. In many countries of the world there are people in detention because their consciences will not allow them to obey the laws of the government. We call them prisoners of conscience.

But what do we mean by conscience? It is simply the individual using his reason to guide him in deciding what is right and what is wrong. He draws upon his knowledge and experience in order to make a moral judgement. Conscience is obviously not an infallible guide and it can be mistaken.

Men's judgements on the same problem will differ widely. Much will depend on how the individual's conscience has been formed. This means that it will depend on such factors as the education he has received, the teaching of the Church to which he may belong, or the various experiences he has had in his own life.

There will be many matters on which an individual will not be capable of making a sound judgement. We cannot have full knowledge of everything.

(a) Must the freedom of the individual to follow his own conscience, even when it is in error, remain supreme in all cases?

Has the State (or any other authority) the right to *force* an individual to admit that his conscience is mistaken?

For example, should an individual citizen be allowed the freedom to refuse vaccination or inoculation, even during an epidemic?

Should he be permitted to commit suicide if he feels his life is no longer worth living?

How far has the State the right to protect its citizens even from themselves?

(b) Do human beings possess an 'instinct' which helps them to choose between right and wrong? Or is it purely a matter of learning and experience?

6 Deviance

*Norm   Anomie   Labelling theory
Culture   Socialisation*

Being yourself

When does it become wrong to be different from other people?

In the following story, Ray Bradbury takes a chilling glimpse into the future. An innocent evening stroll has become a 'regressive tendency'—something which will lead you back into evil ways if it is not corrected. This is simply because an evening stroll is no longer an activity in which other members of society take part. It is no longer the social norm.

In other words, if you persist in being different, you may end up being labelled deviant—one who has fallen into error. And that can call for some action to be taken against you.

The Pedestrian

To enter out into that silence that was the city at eight o'clock of a misty evening in November, to put your feet upon that buckling concrete walk, to step over grassy seams and make your way, hands in pockets, through the silences, that was what Mr Leonard Mead most dearly loved to do. He would stand upon the corner of an intersection and peer down long moonlit avenues of sidewalk in four directions, deciding which way to go, but it really made no difference; he was alone in this world of AD 2052, or as good as alone, and with a final decision made, a path selected, he would stride off, sending patterns of frosty air before him like the smoke of a cigar.

Sometimes he would walk for hours and miles and return only at midnight to his house. And on his way he would see the cottages and homes with their dark windows, and it was not unlike walking through a graveyard where only the faintest glimmers of firefly light appeared in flickers behind the windows. Sudden grey phantoms seemed to manifest upon inner room walls where a curtain was still undrawn against the night, or there were whisperings and murmurs where a window in a tomb-like building was still open.

Mr Leonard Mead would pause, cock his head, listen, look, and march on, his feet making no noise on the lumpy walk. For long ago he had wisely changed to sneakers when strolling at night, because the dogs in intermittent squads would parallel his journey with barkings if he wore hard heels, and lights might click on and faces appear and an entire street be startled by the passing of a lone figure, himself, in the early November evening.

On this particular evening he began his journey in a westerly direction, toward the hidden sea. There was a good crystal frost in the air; it cut the nose and made the lungs blaze like a Christmas tree inside; you could feel the cold light going on and off, all the branches filled with invisible snow. He listened to the faint push of his soft shoes through autumn leaves with satisfaction, and whistled a cold quiet whistle between his teeth, occasionally picking up a leaf as he passed, examining its skeletal pattern in the infrequent lamplights as he went on, smelling its rusty smell.

'Hello, in there,' he whispered to every house on every side as he moved. 'What's up to-night on Channel 4, Channel 7, Channel 9? Where are the cowboys rushing, and do I see the United States Cavalry over the next hill to the rescue?'

The street was silent and long and empty, with only his shadow moving like the shadow of a hawk in mid-country. If he closed his eyes and stood very still, frozen, he could imagine himself upon the centre of a plain, a wintry, windless Arizona desert with no house in a thousand miles, and only dry river beds, the streets, for company.

'What is it now?' he asked the houses, noticing his wrist watch. 'Eight-thirty p.m.? Time for a dozen assorted murders? A quiz? A revue? A comedian falling off the stage?'

Was that a murmur of laughter from within a moon-white house? He hesitated, but went on when nothing more happened. He stumbled over a particularly uneven section of sidewalk. The cement was vanishing under flowers and grass. In ten years of walking by night or day, for thousands of miles, he had never met another person walking, not one in all that time.

He came to a cloverleaf intersection which stood silent where two main highways crossed the town. During the day it was a thunderous surge of cars, the gas stations open, a great insect rustling and a ceaseless jockeying for position as the scarab-beetles, a faint incense puttering from their exhausts, skimmed homeward to the far directions. But now these highways, too, were like streams in a dry season, all stone and bed and moon radiance.

He turned back on a side street circling around toward his home. He was within a block of his destination when the lone car turned a corner quite suddenly and flashed a fierce white cone of light upon him. He stood entranced, not unlike a night moth, stunned by the illumination, and then drawn toward it.

A metallic voice called to him:

'Stand still. Stay where you are! Don't move!'

He halted.

'Put up your hands!'

'But ——' he said.

'Your hands up! Or we'll shoot!'

The police, of course, but what a rare, incredible thing; in a city of three million, there was only *one* police car left, wasn't that correct? Ever since a year ago, 2052, the election year, the force had been cut down from three cars to one. Crime was ebbing; there was no need now for the police, save for this one lone car wandering and wandering the empty streets.

'Your name?' said the police car in a metallic whisper. He couldn't see the men in it for the bright light in his eyes.

'Leonard Mead,' he said.

'Speak up!'

'Leonard Mead!'

'Business or profession?'

'I guess you'd call me a writer.'

'No profession,' said the police car, as if talking to itself. The light held him fixed, like a museum specimen, needle thrust through chest.

'You might say that,' said Mr Mead. He hadn't written in years. Magazines and books didn't sell any more. Everything went on in the tomb-like houses at night now, he thought, continuing his fancy. The tombs, ill-lit by television light, where the people sat like the dead, the grey or multicoloured lights touching their faces, but never really touching *them*.

39

'No profession,' said the phonograph voice, hissing. 'What are you doing out?'

'Walking,' said Leonard Mead.

'Walking!'

'Just walking,' he said simply, but his face felt cold.

'Walking, just walking, walking?'

'Yes, sir.'

'Walking where? For what?'

'Walking for air. Walking to *see*.'

'Your address!'

'Eleven South Saint James Street.'

'And there is air *in* your house, you have an air *conditioner*, Mr Mead?'

'Yes.'

'And you have a viewing screen in your house to see with?'

'No.'

'No?' There was a crackling quiet that in itself was an accusation.

'Are you married, Mr Mead?'

'No.'

'Not married,' said the police voice behind the fiery beam. The moon was high and clear among the stars and the houses were grey and silent.

'Nobody wanted me,' said Leonard Mead with a smile.

'Don't speak unless you're spoken to!'

Leonard Mead waited in the cold night.

'Just *walking*, Mr Mead?'

'Yes.'

'But you haven't explained for what purpose.'

'I explained; for air, and to see, and just to walk.'

'Have you done this often?'

'Every night for years.'

The police car sat in the centre of the street with its radio throat faintly humming.

'Well, Mr Mead,' it said.

'Is that all?' he asked politely.

'Yes,' said the voice. 'Here.' There was a sigh, a pop. The back door of the police car sprang wide. 'Get in.'

'Wait a minute, I haven't done anything!'

'Get in.'

'I protest!'

'Mr Mead.'

He walked like a man suddenly drunk. As he passed the front window of the car he looked in. As he had expected, there was no one in the front seat, no one in the car at all.

'Get in.'

He put his hand to the door and peered into the back seat, which was a little cell, a little black jail with bars. It smelled of riveted steel. It smelled of harsh antiseptic; it smelled too clean and hard and metallic. There was nothing soft there.

'Now if you had a wife to give you an alibi,' said the iron voice. 'But ——'

'Where are you taking me?'

The car hesitated, or rather gave a faint whirring click, as if information, somewhere, was dripping card by punch-slotted card under electric eyes. 'To the Psychiatric Centre for Research on Regressive Tendencies.'

He got in. The door shut with a soft thud. The police car rolled through the night avenues, flashing its dim lights ahead.

They passed one house on one street a moment later, one house in an entire city of houses that were dark, but this one particular house had all of its electric lights brightly lit, every window a loud yellow illumination, square and warm in the cool darkness.

'That's *my* house,' said Leonard Mead.

No one answered him.

The car moved down the empty river-bed streets and off away, leaving the empty streets with the empty sidewalks, and no sound and no motion all the rest of the chill November night.

From *The Golden Apples of the Sun* by Ray Bradbury

The social norm

1 Is it true that any society as a whole will not tolerate those who act differently from the norm?

Ray Bradbury's story is set at some time in the future. But does the same sort of thing happen today? Can you think of examples in our own society of individuals or groups being looked upon as deviant simply because they are different? Consider this question in relation to each of the following points:

(a) race   (b) religion   (c) dress and appearance
(d) cultural activities—for example, music and dance

2 What sort of pressures are put upon us to conform to socially acceptable patterns of life?

What sort of 'punishments' are we likely to incur if we don't conform?

3 How do social norms arise? Why do some forms of behaviour become acceptable in society while other forms are rejected?

Consider the following influences.

(a) daily newspapers
(b) comics, magazines and other periodicals
(c) books
(d) television
(e) wireless
(f) advertising
(g) the cinema
(h) the teaching of churches
(i) education in school
(j) Parliament and legislation
(k) political parties
(l) pressure groups—for example, the women's liberation movement
(m) the example of behaviour given by well-known people in public life
(n) the behaviour of parents and other members of the family circle

Put each of these influences into your own order of importance in respect of

(i) the degree of influence you think they have in making forms of behaviour *socially* acceptable or unacceptable;
(ii) the degree of influence you think they have on your own *personal* behaviour.

Compare results with the rest of your group.

True or false?

4 *Mob rule*

(a) The general public is easily led by the mass media. People can be made to adopt particular opinions without even being aware of it.

(b) We have to cease to conform to public standards of behaviour if we wish to be independent thinkers.

(c) The nature of the world is such there can only be an elite few who govern, and the remainder who must obey.

(d) While we must allow freedom for minority opinions, we are more likely to be right if we follow the views held by the majority.

(e) Intolerance often arises from fear. We see those who think or act differently from us as a threat to an established way of life which we do not want to change.

(f) Peaceful co-existence is not always possible. Some conflicts in society are bound to lead to violence.

Delinquency

5 When does deviance become delinquency? Who makes the judgement? What sort of behaviour in young people would you define as delinquent? Is there any difference between delinquency and crime?

6 Many reasons are often given for the creation of juvenile delinquents, and as many remedies are suggested. Discuss the relative importance of each of the following statements.

Juvenile delinquents

(a) are immature persons who will grow out of it if left alone

(b) are very unhappy young people who need psychological help

(c) are victims of their own inborn weaknesses

(d) have decided to follow their evil tendencies instead of their good ones

(e) often do nothing very bad at all

(f) are created by the degrading conditions in which they are forced to live

(g) are protesting against social injustice in the only way they can

(h) are created by the neglect of parents who should themselves be punished by law for their children's offences

(i) need severe punishment to act as a deterrent to others and to teach them a sense of personal responsibility for their own actions

Deviant or delinquent? How different are we allowed to be?

Points of view

7 Opting out

How far is our way of life an accident of birth? It is obvious that we have no choice with regard to the family, the nation or the period of history into which we are born. But is it easy to opt out—to follow a way of life different from the one we find around us? Consider the following situation:

> John's parents are convinced Christians. He was baptised into the Roman Catholic Church while he was still a baby and he and his parents have always gone to church together each Sunday. Now John is fourteen years old and many of his friends come from families with no Christian faith. He finds the services in church very boring and he no longer feels sure that there is a God. He wants to stop going to church.

(a) How easy do you think it would be for John to opt out? Make a note of the difficulties he might have to face from (a) his parents, (b) his church, or (c) his school.

(b) What should be the attitude of John's parents? Should they allow him to go his own way? Or should they insist that he continues to follow the family's faith, on the grounds that he is not yet old enough to make a valid choice for himself? When would he be old enough to make such a decision? Is it always better to follow your parents' way of life until you are able to leave home?

What do you think?

7 Inequality

Class   Status   Stratification

> The greatness of God is infinite, for while with one die, man impresses many coins and they are all alike, the King of Kings, the Holy One, with one die, he impresses the same image on all men, yet not one of them is like his companions.
>
> *Talmud* (The Jewish Book of Law)

It is perhaps a truism to say in a modern democracy that all men are born different but equal. But then we must ask—Equal in what respect? How do we accept the inequalities we see around us? What causes them? Are they inevitable? Or do they offend against justice, and if so how do we reduce them? These are just some of the questions which must arise.

Social class

One of the chief elements in social inequality, if not the most important one, is social class, which is difficult to define but very easily recognised. The importance of this element in producing divisions within society is stressed by the fact that, when people from different social classes meet, it is difficult for them even to talk to each other—a point well illustrated in the novel *Love Story* by Erich Segal.

Oliver Barrett IV is the son of a wealthy Boston banker. He has come to despise the 'upper' class into which he was born. Whilst at college he meets and falls in love with Jenny Cavilleri, daughter of a typical 'working class' family of Italian origin. Oliver takes Jenny to meet his parents for the first time.

Ipswich, Mass., is some forty minutes from the Mystic River Bridge, depending on the weather and how you drive. I have actually made it on occasion in twenty-nine minutes. A certain distinguished Boston banker claims an even faster time, but when one is discussing sub thirty minutes from Bridge to Barretts', it is difficult to separate fact from fancy. I happen to consider twenty-nine minutes as the absolute limit. I mean, you can't ignore the traffic signals on Route 1 can you?

'You're driving like a maniac,' Jenny said.

'This is Boston,' I replied. 'Everyone drives like a maniac.' We were halted for a red light on Route 1 at the time.

'You'll kill us before your parents can murder us.'

'Listen, Jen, my parents are lovely people.'

The light changed. The MG was at sixty in under ten seconds.

'Even the Sonovabitch?' she asked.

'Who?'

'Oliver Barrett III.'

'Ah, he's a nice guy. You'll really like him.'

'How do you know?'

'Everybody likes him,' I replied.

'Then why don't you?'

'Because everybody likes him,' I said.

Why was I taking her to meet them, anyway? I mean, did I really need Old Stonyface's blessing or anything? Part of it was that she wanted to ('That's the way it's done, Oliver') and part of it was the simple fact that Oliver III was my banker in the very grossest sense: he paid the goddamn tuition.

It had to be Sunday dinner, didn't it? I mean, that's comme il faut, right? Sunday, when all the lousy drivers were clogging Route 1 and getting in my way. I pulled off the main drag onto Groton Street, a road whose turns I had been taking at high speeds since I was thirteen.

'There are no houses here,' said Jenny, 'just trees.'

'The houses are behind the trees.'

When travelling down Groton Street, you've got to be very careful or else you'll miss the turn-off into our place. Actually, I missed the turn-off myself that afternoon. I was three hundred yards down the road when I screeched to a halt.

'Where are we?' she asked.

'Past it,' I mumbled, between obscenities.

Is there something symbolic in the fact that I backed up three hundred yards to the entrance of our place? Anyway, I drove slowly once we were on Barrett soil. It's at least a half mile in from Groton Street to Dover House proper. En route you pass other . . . well, buildings. I guess it's fairly impressive when you see it for the first time.

'Holy shit!' Jenny said.

'What's the matter, Jen?'

'Pull over, Oliver. No kidding. Stop the car.'

I stopped the car. She was clutching.

'Hey, I didn't think it would be like this.'

'Like what?'

'Like this rich. I mean, I bet you have *serfs* living here.'

I wanted to reach over and touch her, but my palms were not dry (an uncommon state), and so I gave her verbal reassurance.

'Please, Jen. It'll be a breeze.'

'Yeah, but why is it I suddenly wish my name was Abigail Adams, or Wendy WASP?'

We drove the rest of the way in silence, parked and walked up to the front door. As we waited for the ring to be answered, Jenny succumbed to a last-minute panic.

'Let's run,' she said.

'Let's stay and fight,' I said.

Was either of us joking?

The door was opened by Florence, a devoted and antique servant of the Barrett family.

'Ah, Master Oliver,' she greeted me.

God, how I hate to be called that! I detest that implicitly derogatory distinction between me and Old Stonyface.

My parents, Florence informed us, were waiting in the library. Jenny was taken aback by some of the portraits we passed. Not just that some were by John Singer Sargent (notably Oliver Barrett II, sometimes displayed in the Boston Museum), but the new realisation that not all of my forebears were named Barrett. There had been solid Barrett *women* who had mated well and bred such creatures as Barrett Winthrop, Richard Barrett Sewall and even Abbott Lawrence Lyman, who had the temerity to go through life (and Harvard, its implicit analogue), becoming a prize-winning chemist, without so much as a Barrett in his middle name!

'Jesus Christ,' said Jenny. 'I see half the buildings at Harvard hanging here.'

'Its all crap,' I told her.

48

'I didn't know you were related to Sewall Boat House too,' she said.

'Yeah. I come from a long line of wood and stone.'

At the end of the long row of portraits, and just before one turns into the library, stands a glass case. In the case are trophies. Athletic trophies.

'They're gorgeous,' Jenny said. 'I've never seen ones that look like real gold and silver.'

'They are.'

'Jesus. Yours?'

'No. His.'

It is an indisputable matter of record that Oliver Barrett III did not place in the Amsterdam Olympics. It is, however, also quite true that he enjoyed significant rowing triumphs on various other occasions. Several. Many. The well-polished proof of this was now before Jennifer's dazzled eyes.

'They don't give stuff like that in the Cranston bowling leagues.'

Then I think she tossed me a bone.

'Do you have trophies, Oliver?'

'Yes.'

'In a case?'

'Up in my room. Under the bed.'

She gave me one of her good Jenny-looks and whispered:

'We'll go look at them later, huh?'

Before I could answer, or even gauge Jenny's true motivations for suggesting a trip to my bedroom, we were interrupted.

'Ah, hello there.'

Sonavabitch! It was the Sonavabitch.

'Oh, hello sir. This is Jennifer—'

'Ah, hello there.'

He was shaking her hand before I could finish the introduction. I noted that he was not wearing any of his Banker Costumes. No indeed; Oliver III had on a fancy cashmere sport jacket. And there was an insidious smile on his usually rocklike countenance.

'Do come in and meet Mrs Barrett.'

Another once-in-a-lifetime thrill was in store for Jennifer: meeting Alison Forbes 'Tipsy' Barrett. (In perverse moments I wondered how her boarding-school nickname might have affected her, had she not grown up to be the earnest do-gooder museum trustee she was.) Let the record show that Tipsy

49

Forbes never completed college. She left Smith in her sophomore year, with the full blessing of her parents, to wed Oliver Barrett III.

'My wife Alison, this is Jennifer—'

He had already usurped the function of introducing her.

'Calliveri,' I added, since Old Stony didn't know her last name.

'Cavilleri,' Jenny added politely, since I had mispronounced it—for the first and only time in my goddamn life.

'As in *Cavalleria Rusticana?*' asked my mother, probably to prove that despite her drop-out status, she was still pretty cultured.

'Right.' Jenny smiled at her. 'No relation.'

'Ah,' said my mother.

'Ah,' said my father.

To which, all the time wondering if they had caught Jenny's humour, I could but add: 'Ah?'

Mother and Jenny shook hands, and after the usual exchange of banalities from which one never progressed in my house, we sat down. Everybody was quiet. I tried to sense what was happening. Doubtless, Mother was sizing up Jennifer, checking out her costume (not Boho this afternoon), her posture, her demeanour, her accent. Face it, the Sound of Cranston was there even in the politest of moments. Perhaps Jenny was sizing up Mother. Girls do that, I'm told. It's supposed to reveal things about the guys they're going to marry. Maybe she was also sizing up Oliver III. Did she notice he was taller than I? Did she like his cashmere jacket?

Oliver III, of course, would be concentrating his fire on me, as usual.

'How've you been, son?'

For a goddamn Rhodes scholar, he is one lousy conversationalist.

'Fine, sir. Fine.'

As a kind of equal-time gesture, Mother greeted Jennifer.

'Did you have a nice trip down?'

'Yes,' Jenny replied, 'nice and swift.'

'Oliver is a swift driver,' interposed Old Stony.

'No swifter than you Father,' I retorted.

What would he say to that?

'Uh—yes. I suppose not.'

You bet your ass not, Father.

50

Mother, who is always on his side, whatever the circumstances, turned the subject to one of more universal interest—music or art, I believe. I wasn't exactly listening carefully. Subsequently, a teacup found its way into my hand.

'Thank you,' I said, then added, 'We'll have to be going soon.'

'Huh?' said Jenny. It seems they had been discussing Puccini or something, and my remark was considered somewhat tangential. Mother looked at me (a rare event).

'But you did come for dinner, didn't you?'

'Uh—we can't,' I said.

'Of course,' Jenny said, almost at the same time.

'I've gotta get back,' I said earnestly to Jen.

Jenny gave me a look of 'What are you talking about?' Then Old Stonyface pronounced:

'You're staying for dinner. That's an order.'

The fake smile on his face didn't make it any less of a command. And I don't take that kind of crap even from an Olympic finalist.

'We can't, sir,' I replied.

'We have to, Oliver,' said Jenny.

'Why?' I asked.

'Because I'm hungry,' she said.

From *Love Story* by Erich Segal

1 What creates social class? Can we identify the elements involved? How does society come to be divided into lower, middle and upper classes? What do we mean by 'working class'?

(a) *Education.* Does our educational system create its own class distinctions or does it merely reflect the ones already in society?

(b) *Opportunity.* What do we mean by equal opportunity? Is it possible for everyone to have equal choices? Do we all have the same aims and ambitions?

(c) *Race and religion.* Do we inherit from our racial or religious backgrounds different cultures and ways of life, which most people passively accept and which tie us to a particular class?

(d) *Politics.* Do the political parties draw their members from particular social classes?

(e) *Occupation.* Will some types of work always be regarded as having higher social prestige and status than others?

(f) *Leisure.* Is there a social class distinction in the way we enjoy ourselves?

(g) *Intelligence.* Are some interests regarded as more 'intellectual', e.g. classical music, grand opera, Shakespearian drama, and therefore of higher social status?

(h) *Money.* Do you need to be rich in order to belong to the 'upper' classes?

(i) *Personality.* Will some people always have an innate desire to be 'superior' to those around them?

(j) *Language.* Do people reveal their social class by the way they speak?

(k) *Dress.* Can you discern social class by the clothes people wear?

2 Put the above factors into your order of importance and compare results. Are there any other elements in the creation of social class which you would add to the list?

Upper class? Or just rich?

Poverty

In the 1930s the removal of poverty was seen as the most important task in creating equality. Writers like George Orwell spoke up for the lower classes.

The train bore me away, through the monstrous scenery of slag-heaps, chimneys, piled scrap-iron, foul canals, paths of cindery mud criss-crossed by the prints of clogs. This was March, but the weather had been horribly cold, and everywhere there were mounds of blackened snow. As we moved slowly through the outskirts of the town we passed row after row of little grey slum houses running at right angles to the embankment. At the back of one of the houses a young woman was kneeling on the stones, poking a stick up the leaden waste-pipe which ran from the sink inside and which I suppose was blocked.

I had time to see everything about her—her sacking apron, her clumsy clogs, her arms reddened by the cold. She looked up as the train passed, and I was almost near enough to catch her eye. She had a round pale face, the usual exhausted face of the slum girl who is twenty-five and looks forty, thanks to miscarriages and drudgery; and it wore, for the second in which I saw it, the most desolate, hopeless expression I have ever seen.

It struck me then that we are mistaken when we say that 'It isn't the same for them as it would be for us', and that people bred in the slums can imagine nothing but the slums. For what I saw in her face was not the ignorant suffering of an animal. She knew well enough what was happening to her—understood as well as I did how dreadful a destiny it was to be kneeling there in the bitter cold, on the slimy stones of a slum backyard, poking a stick up a foul drain-pipe.

From *The Road to Wigan Pier* by George Orwell

3 Today we claim to have an affluent society. The sort of poverty described by George Orwell has been greatly reduced. Is there any evidence that this has produced a more equal society? Is the gap between the upper and lower limits of income still as wide as ever?

4 Consider the following modern social developments. How far
have they helped to bring equality into our lives?

> communal housing projects (e.g. estates, high-rise flats)
> comprehensive schools
> the National Health Service
> the nationalisation of industry
> 'equality' laws (e.g. Acts against sexual and racial discrimi-
> nation)

Difference

5 Here are some kinds of difference between people. Which of
them can be regarded as inevitable and unchangeable?

> sex
> 'natural' talent and ability
> temperament (ambition, desires, likes, dislikes)
> personality (outgoing, open, reserved, placid)
> physical strength
> state of health
> physical or mental disability
> race and culture
> religion and belief
> nationality

6 Are there inequalities which some of the above will produce and
which will always be a part of human life?

Points of view

7 Competition

On 7 December 1889 the people of London flocked to the Savoy
Theatre to see *The Gondoliers*, a new comic opera with words by
William Gilbert and music by Arthur Sullivan. It was the twelfth
opera the two men had written together and it was to become as
famous as all the others. The Gilbert and Sullivan operas are now
known all over the world. Gilbert often used his songs to poke fun
at society, but his comments would have a serious thought behind
them.

In *The Gondoliers* it is proposed to pass laws making everybody equal. One of the characters in the opera has seen that done before and he sings a song about it.

There lived a King, as I've been told,
In the wonder-working days of old,
When hearts were twice as good as gold,
    And twenty times as mellow.

Good temper triumphed in his face,
And in his heart he found a place
For all the erring human race
    And every wretched fellow.

When he had Rhenish wine to drink
It made him very sad to think
That some, at junket or at jink,
    Must be content with toddy.

He wished all men as rich as he
(And he was rich as rich could be),
So to the top of every tree
    Promoted everybody.

Lord Chancellors were cheap as sprats,
And Bishops in their shovel hats
Were plentiful as tabby cats—
    In point of fact, too many.

Ambassadors cropped up like hay,
Prime Ministers and such as they
Grew like asparagus in May,
    And Dukes were three a penny.

On every side Field-Marshalls gleamed,
Small beer were Lords-Lieutenant deemed,
With Admirals the ocean teemed
    All round his wide dominions.

And Party Leaders you might meet
In twos and threes in every street
Maintaining, with no little heat,
    Their various opinions.

That King, although no one denies
His heart was of abnormal size,
Yet he'd have acted otherwise
    If he had been acuter.

The end is easily foretold,
When every blessed thing you hold
Is made of silver, or of gold,
    You long for simple pewter.

When you have nothing else to wear
But cloth of gold and satins rare,
For cloth of gold you cease to care—
    Up goes the price of shoddy.

In short, whoever you may be,
To this conclusion you'll agree,
When every one is somebodee,
    Then no one's anybody!

from *The Gondoliers* by W. S. Gilbert

Following Gilbert we may say that inequality is a necessary part of human society. It makes it possible to have competition, which is a part of our nature. Competition helps us to keep our freedom as individuals. If human beings had nothing to strive for we would be faced with a world of utter boredom. We must not confuse social justice with equality. They are not necessarily the same thing.

What do you think?

8 Faith

How much faith?

Despite the refusal of missionary societies to accept me for
training, I, knowing it was God's will I should go to China, read
the Bible and found that through faith one could do anything.
He kept His promises and it just needed me to take Him at His
word and all would be well.

Gladys Aylward, Christian missionary in China

It would be difficult for anyone to explain why a young parlour-
maid who had never set foot outside her native land, and who had
been rejected as unsuitable for missionary work, should still nurse
within her a burning desire to travel to a remote corner of China in
order to preach the word of God. Yet no one could doubt that
Gladys Aylward had such a desire, and somehow she worked,
scraped and saved in order to fulfil it.

Her story has been told in *The Small Woman* and later in the film,
The Inn of the Sixth Happiness, so that millions of people have now
learned something of her Christian mission and extraordinary
religious faith.

There arrived during her second year at Yangcheng a pleasant
young man called Lu-Yung-Cheng. He was a convert sent from
Tsehchow by Mrs Smith, who said she would pay his salary,
which worked out at ninepence a month. He was useful if only
because he could keep an ear to Yang's romantic interpretation
of the Scriptures. It was about two weeks after he arrived, that
he and Gladys were standing in the courtyard when the messenger from the yamen rushed in waving a piece of scarlet
paper. He gabbled at such a rate that Gladys found it difficult to
understand him.

'What's the paper for, anyway?' she asked Lu-Yung-Cheng.

'It's an official summons from the yamen,' said Lu-Yung-Cheng nervously. 'A riot has broken out in the men's prison.'

Gladys was really not very interested. 'Oh, has it?' she said.

'You must come at once,' said the messenger urgently. 'It is most important!'

Gladys stared at him. 'But what's the riot in the prison got to do with us? It can't have anything to do with my foot inspection.'

'You must come at once!' reiterated the messenger loudly. 'It is an official order.' He hopped from one foot to the other in impatience.

Lu-Yung-Cheng looked at her doubtfully. 'When that piece of red paper arrives from the yamen, you must go.' There was a nervous tremor in his voice.

'All right, *you* go and see what it's all about,' said Gladys. 'It's obviously a man's job. I know nothing about prisons. I've never been in one in my life. Though I really don't see what you're supposed to do.'

She could see from Lu-Yung-Cheng's face that the prospect did not appeal to him.

'Hurry, please hurry!' cried the messenger.

Reluctantly, Lu-Yung-Cheng trailed after him to the door. Gladys watched him reach the opening, take a quick look behind at her, then dodge swiftly to the left as the messenger turned to the right. She could hear the sound of his running feet as he tore down the road.

Within two seconds the messenger discovered his loss. He stormed back through the doorway crying 'Ai-ee-ee!' and shaking his fist in rage. He raced across the courtyard towards Gladys, a little fat man without dignity.

'Now *you* must come,' he shouted. 'This is an official paper. You are ordered to come. You *must* come. Now! With me! If you refuse you will get into trouble!'

'All right,' she said mildly. 'I'll come. I really don't know what's the matter with Lu-Yung-Cheng. He must feel ill or something. But I certainly don't see what a riot in the prison has to do with me . . . .'

They hurried up the road and in through the East Gate. A few yards inside the gate the blank outside wall of the prison flanked the main street. From the other side came an unholy cacophony: screams, shouts, yells, the most horrible noises.

'My goodness!' said Gladys, 'it certainly is a riot, isn't it?'

The Governor of the prison, small, pale-faced, his mouth set into a worried line, met her at the entrance. Behind were grouped half a dozen of his staff.

'We are glad you have come,' he said quickly. 'There is a riot in the prison; the convicts are killing each other.'

'So I can hear,' she said. 'But what am I here for? I'm only the missionary woman. Why don't you send the soldiers in to stop it?'

'The convicts are murderers, bandits, thieves,' said the Governor, his voice trembling. 'The soldiers are frightened. There are not enough of them.'

'I'm sorry to hear that,' said Gladys. 'But what do you expect me to do about it? I don't even know why you asked me to come . . . .'

The Governor took one step forward. 'You must go in and stop the fighting!'

'I must go in . . . !' Gladys's mouth dropped open; her eyes rounded in utter amazement. 'Me! Me go in there! Are you mad! If I went in they'd kill me!'

The Governor's eyes were fixed on her with hypnotic intensity. 'But how can they kill you? You tell everybody that you have come here because you have the living God inside you . . . .'

The words bubbled out of the Governor's mouth, his lips twisted in the acuteness of distress. Gladys felt a small, cold shiver down her back. When she swallowed, her throat seemed to have a gritty texture.

'The—living God?' she stammered.

'You preach it everywhere—in the streets and villages. If you preach the truth, if your God protects you from harm, then you can stop this riot.'

Gladys stared at him. Her mind raced round in bewilderment, searching for some fact that would explain her beliefs to this simple, deluded man. A little cell in her mind kept blinking on and off with an urgent semaphore message: 'It's true! You have been preaching that your Christian God protects you from harm. Fail now, and you are finished in Yangcheng. Discard your faith now, and you discard it for ever!' It was a desperate challenge. Somehow, she had to maintain face. Oh, these stupidly simple people! But how could she go into the prison? Those men—murderers, thieves, bandits, rioting and killing each other inside those walls! By the sounds, louder now, a small human hell had broken loose. How could she . . . .? 'I must try,' she said to herself. 'I must try. O God, give me strength.'

She looked up at the Governor's pale face, knowing that now hers was the same colour. 'All right,' she said. 'Open the door. I'll go in to them.' She did not trust her voice to say any more.

'The key!' snapped the Governor. 'The key, quickly.'

One of his orderlies came forward with a huge iron key. It looked designed to unlock the deepest, darkest dungeon in the world. In the keyhole the giant wards grated loudly; the immense iron-barred door swung open. Literally she was pushed inside. It was dark. The door closed behind her. She heard the great key turn. She was locked in the prison with a horde of raving criminals who by their din sounded as if they had all gone completely insane. A dark tunnel, twenty yards long, stretched before her. At the far end it appeared to open out into a courtyard. She could see figures racing across the entrance. With faltering footsteps, she walked through it and came to an abrupt standstill, rooted in horror.

The courtyard was about sixty feet square, with queer cage-like structures round all four sides. Within its confines a writhing, fiendish battle·was going on. Several bodies were stretched out on the flagstones. One man, obviously dead, lay only a few feet away from her, blood still pouring from a great wound in his scalp. There was blood everywhere. Inside the cage-like structures small private battles were being fought. The main group of men, however, were watching one convict who brandished a large, bloodstained chopper. As she stared, he suddenly rushed at them and they scattered wildly to every part of the square. Gladys stood there, aghast at this macabre form of 'tag'. The man on the ground with the gash in his skull had obviously been well and truly 'tagged'. No one took any notice whatsoever of Gladys. For fully half a minute she stood motionless with not one single cell of her mind operating to solve her dilemma. The man rushed again; the group parted; he singled one man out and chased him. The man ran towards Gladys, then ducked away. The madman with the axe halted only a few feet from her. Without any instinctive plan, hardly realising what she was doing, she took two angry steps towards him.

'Give me that chopper,' she said furiously. 'Give it to me at once!'

The man turned to look at her. For three long seconds the

wild dark pupils staring from bloodshot eyes glared at her. He took two paces forward. Suddenly, meekly, he held out the axe.

From *The Small Woman* by Alan Burgess

Faith and reason

1 Human beings are raised above all other animals by their ability to reason. Any faith, or set of beliefs, to which we hold, must therefore be reasonable. Faith must not cause us to act against our reason. What sort of faith did Gladys Aylward show by entering the prison to stop the riot? Was it reasonable or unreasonable?

(a) It was unreasonable. The prison governor had a distorted view of Christian belief. It is quite obvious in life that being a Christian does not guarantee protection from harm such as physical injury. By entering the prison as she did, Gladys was supporting the error of the governor. She could quite easily have been killed. She was not using her reason. Her action was more fanatical than faithful.

(b) It was reasonable. Christians have faith in the person of Christ as revealed in the Bible. Having faith in Christ means trusting him. If you rely on trust you are bound to take a risk. This is not unreasonable as we take risks in every walk of life. Gladys believed that it was *possible* that she would be kept from injury. She decided to take the risk. It was important that she should not lose face in that eastern society.

2 Faith is often thought of in terms of a religious belief, but is it not also involved in many other aspects of our lives? In what do you have faith?

Would you include any of the following?

the goodness of other people
your own judgement and power of reason
the judgement of people you respect
your natural instinct or intuition
the policies of a political party
the findings of science
the law of averages

3 Do most people think out their beliefs in a reasonable fashion? Or are they more likely to be guided by their feelings? Is a faith based on feelings likely to be stronger or weaker than one based on argument?

Faith and religion

4 Some reasons may be better than others for choosing to hold religious beliefs. Would you consider each of the following to be a valid reason for holding to a particular faith or way of life?

(a) These beliefs bring me comfort and help me to bear the trials of life.
(b) This is the faith into which God allowed me to be born. It is good enough for me.
(c) It is wiser to follow the teaching of an organised Church which has centuries of experience and learning behind it than to trust your own judgements.
(d) I believe in another life because life on this earth does not satisfy my longing for happiness.
(e) I believe in God because I am afraid and want his support in coping with life.
(f) If you are trying to be as good as you can, that is all you need bother about.
(g) You cannot prove or disprove most religious doctrines so one faith is as good as another.
(h) It makes everyone happier if you go along with the opinions of the majority.

5 The following may be said to be the vital questions on human life with which religious faith is concerned:

(a) How did the human race come to exist?
(b) What is the purpose and meaning in human life here and now?
(c) Is death the end of everything, or are we destined for an eternal life beyond the grave?

What do you believe in relation to the above questions?
Why do you think you have adopted these beliefs rather than any others?
Do you think you are likely to change them in the future?

The Angelus by Millet

Does a simple faith belong to an age of ignorance?

An image of God

The Young Man

There is a young man,
who lives in the world of progress.
He used to worship a God,
Who was kind to him.
The God had a long white beard,
He lived in the clouds,
but all the same,
He was close to the solemn child,
who had secretly
shut him up, in a picture book . . . .

63

If he had only known,
that the God in the picture book,
is not an old man in the clouds,
but the seed of life in his soul,
the man would have lived.
And his life would have flowered,
with the flower of limitless joy.

Caryll Houselander

6 What image of God do you have in your own mind? Would you say that it was an adult or a childish image?

Points of view

7 A simple faith

It is no good asking for a simple religion. After all, real things are not simple. They look simple but they are not. The table I am sitting at looks simple: but ask a scientist to tell you what it is really made of—all about the atoms and how the light waves rebound from them and hit my eye and what they do to the optic nerve and what it does to my brain—and, of course, you will find that what we call 'seeing a table' lands you in mysteries and complications which you can hardly get to the end of. A child saying a child's prayer looks simple. And if you are content to stop there, well and good. But if you are not—and the modern world usually is not—if you want to go on and ask what is really happening—then you must be prepared for something difficult.

From Mere Christianity by C. S. Lewis

(a) Do you agree? Has the great increase in our knowledge of the world made it easier or more difficult to accept a religious faith?
(b) Can a religious faith ever be certain?
(c) Do you think it is necessary 'to go on and ask what is really happening' as C. S. Lewis suggests? Or is a simple religion all that most people desire or need?

9 Suffering

Will and motivation   Sacred/secular

The reality of evil

Richard Hillary was a fighter pilot with the Royal Air Force during the Battle of Britain in the summer of 1940. After that battle had been won, he wrote a memorable book describing the life-style of the young men who had fought it.

He tells of his own 'devil-may-care' attitude to life, of his selfishness, of how even the war itself was important to him only in so far as it provided new experiences for him. The world, so Richard Hillary believed at that time, existed solely for what each individual could get out of it.

Day after day he savoured the thrill of aerial combat as he threw his Spitfire around the skies of southern England. Then came his turn to be the hunted instead of the hunter. His plane was shot down in flames over the English Channel. Although badly burned, Hillary managed to get out of the aircraft and parachute into the sea. Luckily, he was seen from the shore and, after a long search, the Margate lifeboat rescued him and rushed him to hospital.

He was terribly disfigured by his burns and months of suffering followed as the surgeons strove, in one operation after another, to repair the damage done to his face and hands. As he describes these months, he tells of the change which was taking place within himself. He was no longer the carefree young man who saw everything, even a world war, as the means of getting the most out of life. The climax came one night when he was out in London on leave from the hospital. He was having a drink in a public bar when an air raid began and the house next door was hit by a bomb. Hillary joined the others in helping to rescue some of the victims buried in the rubble.

We got the child out first. It was passed back carefully and with an odd sort of reverence by the warden, but it was dead. She

65

must have been holding it to her in the bed when the bomb came.

Finally we made a gap wide enough for the bed to be drawn out. The woman who lay there looked middle-aged. She lay on her back and her eyes were closed. Her face, through the dirt and streaked blood, was the face of a thousand working women; her body under the cotton nightdress was heavy. The nightdress was drawn up to her knees and one leg was twisted under her. There was no dignity about that figure.

Around me I heard voices. 'Where's the ambulance?' 'For Christ's sake don't move her!' 'Let her have some air!'

I was at the head of the bed, and looking down into that tired blood-streaked, work-worn face I had a sense of complete unreality. I took the brandy flask from my hip pocket and held it to her lips. Most of it ran down her chin but a little flowed between those clenched teeth. She opened her eyes and reached out her arms instinctively for the child. Then she started to weep. Quite soundlessly, and with no sobbing, the tears were running down her cheeks when she lifted her eyes to mine.

'Thank you, sir,' she said, and took my hand in hers. And then, looking at me again, she said after a pause, 'I see they got you too.' . . .

Her death was unjust, a crime, an outrage, a sin against mankind—weak, inadequate words which even as they passed through my mind mocked me with their futility.

That that woman should so die was an enormity so great that it was terrifying in its implications, in its lifting of the veil on possibilities of thought so far beyond the grasp of the human mind. It was not just the German bombs, or the German Air Force, or even the German mentality, but a feeling of the very essence of anti-life that no words could convey. This was what I had been cursing—in part, for I had recognised in that moment what it was that Peter and the others had instantly recognised as evil and to be destroyed utterly. I saw now that it was not crime; it was Evil itself—something of which until then I had not even sensed the existence.

From *The Last Enemy* by Richard Hillary

When the doctors had finally finished with him, Hillary struggled with great courage to get back to flying duties with the Royal Air Force. Incredibly he succeeded. Then on 8 January 1943, whilst taking part in a night-flying exercise, his plane went into a spin and once more he crashed in flames. This time he did not survive.

1 Richard Hillary recognised 'Evil itself' in the suffering caused to an innocent woman and her baby by enemy bombing. He described it as 'a feeling of the very essence of anti-life that no words could convey'.

What sort of things do you recognise as evil?

Do you agree that this is a feeling rather than something we can describe in words?

2 Here is a list of things which we may say are evils:

war   drought   murder   pain   flood   famine
sickness   road accident   theft   earthquake   death
racial prejudice   torture   poverty   unemployment
violence   jealousy

Can you add any more to the list?

Are these things always evil?

Good may come out of evil. What good may come out of the above? Are there any from which no good could possibly come?

3 How many of the above evils are manmade, that is, caused by the action of human beings?

How many are natural, that is, they just happen to be present in our world?

Free will

4 There is one sense in which the presence of evil is necessary. We could never recognise 'good' if we did not also know 'evil'. We can say that manmade evils are our own fault and result from the free will of human beings. If we were not free to do evil we would not be free to do good. We can be noble, generous, courageous and immensely lovable—or we can be cruel, greedy, hateful, low and contemptible. It is this freedom to choose between good and evil which makes us infinitely higher than the animals—or infinitely lower. The choice is ours.

Do you agree?

5 Can we explain the presence of the 'natural' evils in the world and the suffering they cause to the innocent?

War

6 Some people regard war as the greatest evil in the world. Do
you think there is a greater one?

Where is the glory of war?

7 Do we glorify war and help it to continue by stressing the courage of those taking part and the glory of the victories they win?

> Cannon to right of them,
> Cannon to left of them,
> Cannon behind them
>   Volley'd and thunder'd;
>
> Storm'd at with shot and shell,
> While horse and hero fell,
> They that had fought so well
> Came thro' the jaws of Death,
> Back from the mouth of Hell,
> All that was left of them,
>   Left of six hundred.
>
> When can their glory fade?
> O the wild charge they made!
>   All the world wonder'd.
> Honour the charge they made!
> Honour the Light Brigade,
>   Noble six hundred!

From 'The Charge of the Light Brigade' by Tennyson

Or do we need to concentrate more on the horrors of war?

> By sundown we came to a hidden village
> Where all the air was still
> And no sound met our tired ears, save
> For the sorry drip of rain from blackened trees
> And the melancholy song of swinging gates.
> . . .
> No one had told us victory was like this;
> Not one amongst us would have eaten bread
> Before he'd filled the mouth of the grey child
> That sprawled, stiff as stone, before the shattered door.
> There was not one who did not think of home.

From 'Conquerors' by Henry Treece

True or false?

8 *Violence and war*

   (a) War can never solve anything. It is an act of self-destruction which creates even more problems.
   (b) War is a necessary last resort as an act of self-defence.
   (c) Wars are inevitable because of the violent and evil nature of mankind.
   (d) If we wish to avoid war, we must eliminate all forms of violence in our own society.
   (e) Boxing is one form of violence which should be banned.
   (f) No act of physical violence is ever justified.
   (g) Ordinary citizens could make it clear to their governments that they will always refuse to fight the ordinary citizens of another country.
   (h) Playing at war games helps young children to get rid of their feelings of aggression in a harmless way.
   (i) In war, no nation ever has all the right on its side.

Points of view

9 *Attitudes to suffering*

   (a) The Welsh poet, Dylan Thomas, standing by the death-bed of his father, was filled with a sense of rage. He saw the suffering of death as an enemy to be fought with all one's might.

> And you, my father, there on the sad height,
> Curse, bless me now with your fierce tears, I pray.
> Do not go gentle into that good night.
> Rage, rage against the dying of the light.

All suffering should fill us with a rage to fight against it. To accept it as 'the will of God' may lessen the effort we make to remove it. In fact, the presence in the world of that suffering which is not caused by man is itself an argument against the existence of an all-powerful, all-good God. How could such a God have created a world in which even the young and innocent may have to endure great suffering? Our only real hope for the future is to put our strength into the fight to remove all forms of suffering from *this* world, here and now.

Those who run away, run
away from their suffering,
take it with them.

It runs alongside, behind,
in front, attached to them
as their shadows are.

Those who stay with it, stay
and find it change
into a gift someday, some

day it is a gift that brings
tears of gratitude.
Do not wriggle, squirm,

scream or shout or run
or blame anything or anyone;
just sit and say

So this, so this is suffering. Lord,
let us lighten thus
Your burden a little.

William Hart-Smith

The quiet acceptance of suffering brings peace of mind. No
matter how hard we fight, there are many forms of suffering
which we cannot remove, and never will. We may do what
we can to make things better, but, in the end, we have to
learn to live with suffering, even when there seems to be no
justice in it. Despite centuries of thought and study, no one
has yet been able to explain why the innocent sometimes
have to suffer. But the hope of a good God and a future life
in which all wrongs will be righted, does, at least, give a
meaning to such lives. If there is no explanation, then the
lives of countless sufferers have been a mockery of existence. Why should they be the unlucky ones?

What do you think?

10 Love

Situation definition   Rationalisation
Motivation

Kinds of love

The desire to love and to be loved is perhaps the most fundamental need of all human beings. This deeply felt psychological need is frequently the motive, either conscious or unconscious, for the way in which we seek our happiness.

The manner in which we express our love depends upon the relationship involved. Each relationship requires its own form of love whether it is between husband and wife, parents and children, relations, friends, strangers, or even enemies.

Ernest Gordon was an officer in the Argyll and Sutherland Highlanders who was captured by the Japanese in 1943 after the fall of Singapore. He spent the next two and a half years as a prisoner in the Far East and had to endure all the horrors of the Japanese prisoner-of-war camps and work on the infamous 'Railway of Death' in Northern Burma. He describes it in his book, *Miracle on the River Kwai.*

Towards the spring of 1943, the Japanese grew increasingly nervous that the railway wouldn't be finished on time, and vented their anxiety on us. Somewhere the guards had picked up the word 'Speedo'. They stood over us with their vicious staves of bamboo yelling 'Speedo! Speedo!', until 'Speedo!' rang in our ears and haunted our sleep. We nicknamed the project 'Operation Speedo'.

When we did not move fast enough to suit them—which was most of the time—they beat us mercilessly. Many no longer had the stamina to endure such beatings. They slid to the ground and died.

Gordon was one of the lucky ones who survived. He tells us how, in 1945, as the war was coming to its end and the Japanese Army facing defeat, he and his fellow-prisoners were transported to another area.

Farther on, we were shunted on to a siding for a lengthy stay. We found ourselves on the same track with several car-loads of Japanese wounded. They were on their own and without medical care. No longer fit for action, they had been packed into railway trucks which were being returned to Bangkok. Whenever one of them died en route, he was thrown off into the jungle. The ones who survived to reach Bangkok would presumably receive some form of medical treatment there. But they were given none on the way.

They were in a shocking state; I have never seen men filthier. Their uniforms were encrusted with mud, blood and excrement. Their wounds, sorely inflamed and full of pus, crawled with maggots. The maggots, however, in eating the putrefying flesh, probably prevented gangrene.

We could understand now why the Japanese were so cruel to their prisoners. If they didn't care a tinker's damn for their own, why should they care for us?

The wounded men looked at us forlornly as they sat with their heads resting against the carriages waiting fatalistically for death. They were the refuse of war; there was nowhere to go and no one to care for them. These were the enemy, more cowed and defeated than we had ever been.

Without a word, most of the officers in my section unbuckled their packs, took out part of their ration and a rag or two, and, with water canteens in their hands went over to the Japanese train to help them. Our guards tried to prevent us, bawling, 'No goodka! No goodka!' But we ignored them and knelt by the side of the enemy to give them food and water, to clean and bind up their wounds, to smile and say a kind word. Grateful cries of 'Aragatto!' ('Thank you!') followed us when we left.

An Allied officer from another section of the train had been taking it all in. 'What bloody fools you all are!' he said to me. 'Don't you realise that those are the enemy?'

From *Miracle on the River Kwai* by Ernest Gordon

1 What is the difference between loving people and liking them?

2 Can you love everyone? Does loving your enemies mean that you have to make friends of them all? What is the best attitude to adopt towards someone you meet for the first time and for whom you feel an immediate dislike?

3 What is the difference between showing affection and showing love? Does physical attraction always lead to love? Does loving someone always make you feel good?

4 Here is one definition of love: 'The sacrifice of oneself for the good of another.' Can you think of a better one? How would *you* decide whether or not one person really loved another?

5 How can the following people express their love for one another?

> brothers and sisters
> children and parents
> husbands and wives
> couples engaged to be married
> friends
> pupils and teachers
> neighbours

6 Is everyone capable of showing love to the same degree? Is loving others a question of maturity? Do we become capable of less selfish love as we grow older?

7 Can human beings be happy on their own without any love for anyone else in their lives at all?

Sexual love

In the novel from which the following extract is taken, Jane Graham has had a brief affair with a boy friend whilst on holiday. She becomes desperately afraid that, as a result, she may have become pregnant, and decides that she must consult someone. Having no regular doctor of her own, she makes an appointment with one of whom she has vaguely heard, without being able to remember in what connection. She is horrified to discover that the doctor has assumed that she has come to arrange an abortion.

I was watching him now, really looking at him carefully. He was so clean and bland and well-fed. Outside, beyond the lace curtains, I could hear the genteel traffic purring along Wimpole Street. It seemed impossible, and yet it was real, it was actually happening.

'How much is the fee?' I asked. I was suddenly so interested I could hardly wait to know.

Dr Graham took off his glasses again and looked at me with his small short-sighted eyes.

'A hundred guineas,' he said.

Then he took out a cream silk handkerchief to polish the lenses. I could see his monogram on the corner, J. G., the same initials as mine.

I stood up and the room rocked for a moment. I felt a bubble of nausea come up into my throat. I closed my eyes, and swallowed, and felt better. I picked up my coat which was over the back of the chair.

'Where are you going?' the doctor asked sharply.

I held on to the back of the chair and looked at him. There was so much to say that I couldn't find words for any of it.

'Well now, look here,' he said in an altered voice. 'I can quite see it might be difficult for you to get hold of a lump-sum like that, especially if you can't turn to the man for help. I'm always so afraid of what you silly little girls will rush off and do to yourselves . . . You must realise I have certain basic costs to meet, but in the special circumstances I can waive my own fee, and my colleague would do the same, I'm sure. Let's say sixty guineas all-in. There, what could be fairer than that?'

My mind was suddenly as cold and clear as ice water. I said, 'One thing could be.'

'What's that?'

'You could make some effort to find out whether I'm really pregnant before you charge me sixty guineas for an operation that might not even be necessary.'

His face didn't change, but his hands paused about the business of polishing his lenses.

'You might even stop to ask me if I want to get rid of my baby, if there is a baby.' I clutched the back of the chair with both hands. I could feel a fever of shaking beginning in my wrists and knees. 'But I suppose when all those guineas are at stake, nothing else seems very important.'

My indignation burned me like a purifying fire. I stared at

the doctor with triumph. My accusation, I thought, was magnificent, unanswerable. I forgot my own guilt in the enormity of his.

He put his glasses back on slowly and tucked his handkerchief away in his breast pocket. Then he leaned on his elbows and looked up at me.

'You want to have your baby?' he asked curiously.

'I wouldn't have chosen to have one this way. But if it's happened, yes, I want it. Anything's better than your cheating way out.'

He looked at the snowy blotter between his elbows.

'Don't, please, misunderstand what I'm going to say. I'm not trying to persuade you to change your mind. In fact, I couldn't have you in my clinic after what you've just said—the risk would be too great. But I wonder how much thought you've given to the child. A lot of the women who come to me aren't just panic-stricken cowards trying to escape their just deserts, you know. They have the sense to realise they're incapable of being mother *and* father, breadwinner *and* nursemaid, all at once. A lot of them have thought what the alternative means, of handing the child over to strangers who may or may not love it. And don't make the mistake of imagining the word bastard doesn't carry a sting any more. There aren't many illegitimate children in this world who haven't, some time or other, thought unkindly of their mothers.'

'How many of them do you suppose honestly wish they'd never been born?'

He looked at me for a long time, and then shrugged. He seemed tired, suddenly: 'I don't know,' he said. 'Life is precious, once you have the realisation of it; even the vilest sort of existence can seem better than nothing. But I think a woman, when she finds she's going to bring a human being into the world, has the right to judge in advance.'

'Well, I don't. That's sheer sophistry. Those women are rationalising their own fear. They're judging for themselves, not for the child.'

'Possibly, in some cases. It's not for me to say.'

'Yours not to reason why, yours but to do—and collect a hundred guineas.'

He smiled wryly. 'There really are overheads involved in doing the thing properly, you know,' he said without anger. 'For me, too, it's a question of considering the alternatives. If

76

there weren't men like me to come to, I wonder how many more deaths there would be following abortions . . .'

'That's a rationalisation, too.'

'Tell me something,' said the doctor gently. 'How did you rationalise your acts of fornication?'

'There was only one,' I said.

I sat down again on the chair because my knees wouldn't hold me any longer. My coat slipped off my arm on to the floor. Without warning the tears came, and ran down my face in streams. I couldn't stop them. There was a great weakness in my whole body; nothing seemed to matter except the enormous sadness of the fact that that one raw, mismanaged, unhappy night could result in this, this misery, this huge frightening vista opening in front of me, this mountain of responsibility. That so little—a wrong decision, and two inept, unsatisfactory performances of the sexual act, which gave so little pleasure—could result in a changed world. As I wept I wondered, foolishly and pointlessly, which of the acts had conceived the child—the first with its bungling and pain and apologies, or the second with its cold frantic struggle to achieve or give the pleasure which might have begun to justify either of them . . .

I felt the doctor's banana hands on my shoulders, and the cream silk handkerchief was put into my hand. 'Don't get so upset,' he said. 'I know it seems bad now, and unfair and all the rest of it, and there'll be moments when you'll wish you'd done what I thought you'd come here for, but there are compensations too. How old are you—26, 27? It's time you had a baby. You're old enough to appreciate it. If you've got the courage to enjoy some of it, it'll do you good.'

When I stopped crying he gave me a drink of sherry and some addresses. It was all suddenly matter-of-fact again, as if he were an employment agency giving me addresses of jobs, but actually they were for an ante-natal clinic, the Society for Unmarried Mothers, and a general practitioner in Hammersmith. He told me the names of books to get out of the library. I wrote everything down carefully on a sheet of paper he gave me. It had his name and degrees printed at the top in small, discreet lettering. When I offered to pay him he wouldn't accept anything. I came away feeling that we had had a battle, and that he'd won.

From *The L-Shaped Room* by Lynne Reid-Banks

8 What is the difference between 'having sex' and 'making love'?

9 Is the act of sexual intercourse necessary to the expression of genuine love between a man and a woman?

10 What sort of commitment, if any, do you think is necessary for a sexual relationship between two people to be a happy one?

11 The laws on abortion have always been the subject of much controversy. There are three main points of view:

(a) Abortion, at whatever time and for whatever reason, is the taking of an innocent life and is wrong. It should be forbidden by law.
(b) A woman should never have to give birth to a child she does not want. She should be allowed by law to have an abortion whenever she requests one.
(c) The decision is not one for the mother alone. The law should state the circumstances in which abortion may be permitted.

What does the law allow today?

Do you agree?

True or false?

12 *Why marriage?*

(a) The difficulties with which unmarried mothers have to contend are a punishment for their sin.
(b) If an unmarried girl becomes pregnant she should marry the father of the child.
(c) Modern methods of contraception make it possible to have sexual intercourse without any fear of having a baby.
(d) An unborn child in the womb has just as much right to life as any other human being.
(e) In casual sexual relationships the woman is always likely to suffer far more than the man.
(f) Sexual attraction is always present in any friendship between boys and girls.
(g) The sexual relationship is the most important part of marriage.

(h) Parents are the best people to give sex education to their children.
(i) Adequate preparation for married life cannot be given in schools.

Seeking pleasure? Or showing love?

Points of view

13 *Sex and life*

(a) The desire for sexual intercourse is part of our nature. There is nothing wrong with two people having a sexual relationship as long as they use a reliable method of contraception. They are satisfying a natural need and are not doing anyone any harm. If this is what they both want, why should they restrain themselves?

(b) The sexual act is not only physical—it involves the mind and the emotions as well. People can seriously harm their emotional development by casual sexual encounters. Sex should be far more than the mere use of another person's body for pleasure. It only brings true happiness and fulfilment if it is part of a personal and exclusive relationship between two people who love each other.

(c) Sex is made into a god by the society we live in. Its joys and pleasures are exaggerated and exploited by the mass media, often for purely commercial reasons. This misleads people into thinking that an active sex life is necessary for human happiness. It is not. Throughout the ages people have had to curb their sexual instincts for a variety of very good reasons. They have nevertheless lived happy and fulfilled lives.

What do you think?

11 Happiness

Self-image   Reference group

What a delight it is
When, of a morning,
I get up and go out
To find in full bloom a flower
That yesterday was not there.

Tachibana Akemi, 'Poems of Solitary Delights'

What is happiness?

Flora Thompson was born in the year 1876 in a small village in Oxfordshire. In her later life she wrote about her upbringing in the English countryside of that time. Her book, *Lark Rise to Candleford*, has become a classic account of life in rural England. She writes of herself as a young woman called Laura who, at the age of thirteen, began to feel that life held no promise of any kind. She began to think of herself as useless and incapable of finding an occupation once she had left school.

All that winter Laura went on with her brooding. Then spring came and the bluebells were out and the chestnut candles and young bracken fronds were unrolling; but, for the first time since she could remember, she had no joy in such things. She sat one day on the low-hanging bough of a beech and looked at them all. 'Here I am,' she thought, 'and here are all these lovely things and I don't care for them a bit this year. There must be something the matter with me.'

There was. She was growing up, and growing up, as she feared, into a world that had no use for her. She carried this burden of care for months, not always conscious of it; some-

81

times she would forget, and in the reaction become noisy and boisterous; but it was always there, pressing down upon her, until the neighbours noticed her melancholy expression and said: 'That child looks regular hag-rid.'

This accumulated depression of months slid from her at last in a moment. She had run out into the fields one day in a pet and was standing on a small stone bridge looking down on brown running water flecked with cream-coloured foam. It was a dull November day with grey sky and mist. This little brook was scarcely more than a trench to drain the fields; but overhanging it were thorn bushes with a lacework of leafless twigs; ivy had sent trails down the steep banks to dip in the stream, and from every thorn on the leafless twigs and from every point of the ivy leaves, water hung in bright drops, like beads.

A flock of starlings had whirred up from the bushes at her approach and the 'clip, clop' of a cart-horse's hoofs could be heard on the nearest road, but these were the only sounds. Of the hamlet, only a few hundred yards away, she could hear no sound, or see as much as a chimney-pot, walled in as she was by the mist.

Laura looked and looked again. The small scene, so commonplace and yet so lovely, delighted her. It was so near the homes of men and yet so far removed from their thoughts. The fresh green moss, the glistening ivy, and the reddish twigs with their sparkling drops seemed to have been made for her alone and the hurrying, foam-flecked water seemed to have some message for her. She felt suddenly uplifted. The things which had troubled her troubled her no more. She did not reason. She had already done plenty of reasoning. Too much, perhaps. She simply stood there and let it all sink in until she felt that her own small affairs did not matter. Whatever happened to her, this, and thousands of other such small, lovely sights would remain and people would come suddenly upon them and look and be glad.

A wave of pure happiness pervaded her being, and, although it soon receded, it carried away with it her burden of care. Her first reaction was to laugh aloud at herself. What a fool she had been to make so much of so little. There must be thousands like her who could see no place for themselves in the world, and here she had been, fretting herself and worrying others as if her case were unique. And, deeper down, beneath the surface of her being, was the feeling, rather than the knowledge, that her life's deepest joys would be found in such scenes as this.

From *Lark Rise to Candleford* by Flora Thompson

1 Many people, like the young Flora Thompson, find a deep sense of happiness in the natural surroundings of the countryside.
What sort of things make you feel happy?
What has been the happiest time of your life so far?

2 Can we think too much about things? Is happiness more related to our feelings than to our reason?

3 Do you think it is easier to live a happy life in the countryside than in a town or city?

4 What is the difference between happiness and pleasure? Do they go together? Does pleasure always bring happiness?

5 What are the essentials of happiness? Put the following points into your order of importance and compare results in your group:

(a) success in some part of our lives
(b) ability to afford some of the luxuries of life
(c) a wide circle of good friends
(d) a job you enjoy doing
(e) an easy conscience and a peaceful mind
(f) independence—not having to rely on others
(g) a settled home and family life
(h) to be able to forget oneself and think of others
(i) good health
(j) to love or be loved by someone else
(k) to be able to count one's blessings and be free from envy
(l) to be well thought of by other people

The pursuit of happiness

We hold these truths to be self-evident, that all men are created equal, that they are endowed by their Creator with certain inalienable rights, that among these are life, liberty, and the pursuit of happiness.

The American Declaration of Independence, 4 July 1776

WAKE WORRY EAT WORRY WORK

WORRY LOVE WORRY FUN RETRIBUTION

How does happiness fit in?

6 How do we set about making the pursuit of happiness our aim in life?

7 Alexander Solzhenitsyn suffered for many years in a Siberian labour camp. He has written about that experience in his book *One Day in the Life of Ivan Denisovich*. This is how the book finishes, as Ivan Denisovich Shukhov climbs into his bunk at the end of a typical day of hardship in the camp.

Shukhov went to sleep fully content. He'd had many strokes of luck that day: they hadn't put him in the cells; they hadn't sent the team to the settlement; he'd pinched a bowl of kasha at dinner; the team-leader had fixed the rates well; he'd built a wall and enjoyed doing it; he'd smuggled that bit of hacksaw-blade through; he'd earned something from Tsezar in the evening; he'd bought that tobacco. And he hadn't fallen ill. He'd got over it.

A day without a dark cloud. Almost a happy day.

From *One Day in the Life of Ivan Denisovich*
by Alexander Solzhenitsyn

Is happiness mainly a question of our attitude of mind?

Can we be happy anywhere and in all circumstances? Is it always our own fault if we are not happy?

8 Millions of people do the football pools each week. Yet some big winners have found only misery. Can we be sure that we know what is best for our own happiness?

Points of view

9 The end of the search

The pursuit of happiness is the mainspring of everybody's life. In everything we do we seek what we think will make us happy. Sometimes we will accept unhappiness but only because of some other advantage to be gained. We may, for example, continue in a job which we dislike. We do it because the money we earn enables us to seek happiness in some other aspect of our lives.

We may sacrifice ourselves for others but we hope to gain their love or affection in return. We may simply wish to serve the God in whom we believe. In this case we hope to gain the eventual happiness of heaven.

In the pursuit of happiness we are bound to be selfish. No sane person would willingly seek misery. There must be some element of personal happiness in everything we do.

We cannot, however, command happiness. If we seek it directly we may never find it. It comes to us as a by-product of our way of life.

What do you think?

Acknowledgements

Acknowledgements and thanks are due to the following authors, publishers and agents for permission to reproduce copyright material.

George Allen & Unwin (Publishers) Ltd, from *Back to Tristan* by Arne Falk-Rønne; Angus & Robertson, Australia, for 'Via Crucis' from *The Talking Clothes: Poems by William Hart-Smith;* Chatto & Windus Ltd, from *The L-Shaped Room* by Lynne Reid-Banks; Collins Publishers, from *Miracle on the River Kwai* by Ernest Gordon, and from *Mere Christianity* by C. S. Lewis; J. M. Dent, Trustees for the copyrights of the late Dylan Thomas, and David Higham Associates Ltd for lines from 'Do Not Go Gentle into that Good Night' from *Collected Poems* by Dylan Thomas; Evans Bros. Ltd, from *The Small Woman* by Alan Burgess; Faber and Faber Ltd for lines from 'Prayer Before Birth' from *The Collected Poems of Louis MacNeice*, and from 'Conquerors' from *The Haunted Garden* by Henry Treece; Samuel French Ltd, from *Spring and Port Wine* by Bill Naughton; Victor Gollancz Ltd, from *One day in the Life of Ivan Denisovich* by Alexander Solzhenitsyn; Wm Heinemann Ltd, the Estate of the late Mrs Frieda Lawrence Ravagli, and Lawrence Pollinger Ltd for lines from 'All That We Have Is Life' from *The Complete Poems of D. H. Lawrence;* Heinemann Educational Books Ltd, from *A Man For All Seasons* by Robert Bolt; Hodder and Stoughton Ltd and Anthony Sheil Associates Ltd, from *Love Story* by Erich Segal; The Hogarth Press Ltd, from *Cider with Rosie* by Laurie Lee; Michael Joseph Ltd, from *A Kestrel for a Knave* by Barry Hines; McGraw-Hill Book Company, from *People I Have Loved, Known or Admired* by Leo Rosten; Macmillan, from *The Last Enemy* by Richard Hillary, and from *Tess of the D'Urbervilles* by Thomas Hardy; Macmillan and David Higham Associates Ltd for 'Timothy Winters' from *Collected Poems* by Charles Causley; Oxford University Press, from *The Sociological Imagination* by C. Wright Mills and from *Lark Rise to Candleford* by Flora Thompson; Penguin Books Ltd for lines from *Poems of Solitary Delights* by Tachibana Akemi from *The Penguin Book of Japanese Verse;* A. D. Peters & Co. Ltd and Hart-Davis MacGibbon Ltd for 'The Pedestrian' from *The Golden Apples of the Sun* by Ray Bradbury; Martin Secker & Warburg Ltd, Mrs Sonia Brownell Orwell and A. M. Heath & Co. Ltd, from *The Road to Wigan Pier* by George Orwell; Sheed and Ward Ltd for lines from the poem 'The Young Man' from *The Flowering Tree* by Caryll Houselander.

Thanks are also due to the following copyright holders for permission to reproduce illustrations.

Page 15, Colin Jones/Camera Press; 19, 22, 79, Jon Blau/Camera Press; 27, Brian Darby/Camera Press; 30, National Portrait Gallery; 44, *Daily Telegraph;* 52, Tim Graham/Camera Press; 63, Musée du Louvre, Paris; 68, Martin Gershen/Camera Press; 84, Jules Feiffer and Shanks, Davis & Remer, N.Y.